The "Biggie" and Other One-Act Plays
by Albert Meglin

stage plays

STAGEPLAYS THEATRE COMPANY
1674 Broadway, Suite 401
New York, New York 10019
Telephone: (212) 354-7565
Telefax: (212) 354-7585
www.stageplaystheatre.com

The "Biggie" and Other One-Act Plays by Albert Meglin
ISBN 0-9754851-4-8

Published by Stageplays Theatre Company

Design, Layout & Photograph: Doug Barron

First Edition, January 2009

Printed in the United States of America

BY WAY OF INTRODUCTION

When I was in junior high school, a friend showed me the book he was reading. It was like no book I had seen before. It was very skinny. Inside, there were no descriptions of trees or hillsides. No sentences began with "He thought" and no clauses like "Suddenly he remembered" or "Four years passed" connected events. What was there? Only conversation. People spoke to each other, revealing things through talk, affecting other people strictly through the force of that talk.

What my friend had introduced me to was, of course, the rewards offered by plays in print. I learned only later – I was a naive Brooklyn boy, after all – that plays were meant to be performed, live, before audiences. But that seemed almost an afterthought, a sort of bonus: by then, I had fallen in love with plays as a reading experience.

I didn't realize it at the time but I had also fallen in love with a craft, a craft of singular and magnificent artifice. The artifice began with three walls, and not very sturdy walls at that, which could represent a living room or a barnyard or a ship's engine room. Things happened in those living rooms and barnyards and engine rooms. People – dramatists – made things happen there. And if they did their job well, they made other people – audiences – believe in those things absolutely. Remarkable! One day, I hoped, I might learn this astonishing craft!

Later still, I came to admire a more exacting, more compressed version of this craft: the one-act play. I began to – well, perhaps I'll leave all that for Volume Two.

I hope you enjoy reading the plays in this book.

A. M.

contents

THE "BIGGIE"

a one-act play

The "Biggie"

setting:

Rialto Room, the smallest and most romantic of the restaurants on the Crystal Harmony cruise ship.

At center stage, a small bistro table and two chairs. This is the corner table where the romantic hijinks take place.

At the left, a more secluded table with one chair, where staff member MISS JULIE will try to dine when her duties for the evening permit. At one frustrating point, she will trot out a 3-panel screen to afford herself a bit of privacy while she eats.

time:
The present, an evening in summer.

characters:

Miss Julie: social director for this singles event, 40-ish, experienced, energetic, upbeat and relentlessly cheerful. Actually, she is over-the-top: her job demands it. Her white satin suit is over-the-top, her white satin heels are over-the-top, and even the large white flower at her throat is over-the-top.

Estrella Morrison: single at 36 and moderately, very moderately, pretty. A bookkeeper by trade, she requires release; she gets it by doing a full repertoire of imitations, her arsenal of weapons in her desire for social acceptance.

Mitchell Bernard Wykoff: (also known as BERNARD MITCHELL WYKOFF) 38, shy, balding, clumsy, anal-retentive. He is an accountant for the 4th largest car rental firm east of the Mississippi, and he is still suffering from the fact that his erstwhile girlfriend ditched him as "boring". He is the last person in the world who would do imitations.

Before closed curtains, a spotlighted MISS JULIE, *microphone in hand, addresses the singles in front of her.*

MISS JULIE: Welcome, welcome, Crystal Harmony cruisers, especially you singles, which is all of you, or why would you be joining us tonight for the big Crystal Harmony Cruises Computer Pair-Up? Yes, yes! This is Miss Julie, your Miss Julie, hostess *extraordinaire*, as my French friends say. You will shortly enter the Rialto Room, your Rialto Room, for our evening festivities. Love is in the air, my dear ones!

Clicking off the microphone, SHE *turns and addresses the audience.*

So? It's all cowflop, so what? It's what they want to hear, right? Listen, a secret, okay? On board? The biggest bunch of weirdos we have ever had! No, I mean it! Each and every one, a major creep! *"Gornish helfen,"* as my Jewish friends say, "nothing will help!" Still, Miss Julie's credo is: hope springs eternal. She will get this show on the right road!

Clicking on the microphone, SHE *turns and addresses the singles.*

You, my dear ones, did your part yesterday, did you not, filling out your Crystal Harmony Love Lists, dutifully and truthfully, one hopes, ha, ha, answering all 14 subtle but instructive questions, yes? "The holidays I love most are dash-dash…the travel spots I love most are dash-dash… the songs," *etc., etc.* Predictors of compatibility each and every one. Ah, and the best predictor of all, the one your Miss Julie calls "The Big Question," or "The Biggie," for short – yes, question #14: "The life partner I love most will dash-dash, big dash-dash," yes!

Clicking off the microphone, SHE *turns and addresses the audience.*

You wouldn't believe, you would not believe, the answers on some of these Love Lists. Losers, I tell you, losers all! Still, there will be romance tonight, and it will ignite at that table in the corner. Ask me how I know! One sec and I'll spill you some beans.

Clicking on the microphone, SHE *turns and addresses the singles.*

And how has your Miss Julie managed your Love Lists? With a little help from her faithful assistant, Juanito, she has spent all of last night, I mean all of it, at the infallible Crystal Harmony computer, entering your data, correlating, making sure your dinner tonight is in the company of the soul mate of your dreams, the one person on board whose Love List best matches your own. Yes! Am I permitted to say all that was not easy! Who taught you guys penmanship? King Kong? Ha, ha! Pay no mind: Miss Julie is only funnin', as my friends from the deep South are known to say.

Clicking off the microphone, SHE *turns and addresses the audience.*

Listen, another secret, okay? That "infallible Crystal Harmony computer?" It's been down all week and no sign of a repair! Miss Julie did everything by hand last night, all last night, which is why she is altogether done in! So, anyway, that corner table? Their Love Lists?

A perfect match! I kid you not! Every one of the 14 questions answered exactly the same, in exactly the same words – favorite books, favorite foods, favorite everything! Incredible! *In-cray-ible!* Oh – and also: they are Looneybirds! I still kid you not. Here's "The Biggie" – are you ready? They both want a life partner who will – I'm quoting here! – "recognize and respect my imitations". You heard correctly. You have heard correctly! They are imitators, both of them. They do imitations!

No attempt at BETTE DAVIS here.

"Fasten your seat belts, it's going to be a–" that sort of thing. Yes! Scout's honor! One sec and I'll tell you more.

Clicking on the microphone, SHE *turns and addresses the singles.*

Cruisers! You have received your table assignment, have you not? Get ready for a lovely 15-minute "Meet-and-Greet" period with your Pair-Up – our version of foreplay, some call it, ha, ha! Next, Juanito will come to you with your matched Love Lists, your pleasures, guilty or otherwise, laid bare, so to speak, for you to consider, compare, and corroborate, for congenial compatibility. Miss Julie is in high C tonight, ha, ha!

Clicking off the microphone, SHE *turns and addresses the audience.*

Are you ready for their "Biggies?" Are you?

Referring to the Love Lists in hand.

Here's Ms. Female Looneybird, who, by the way, called on me 40 times today to remind me her life partner must "recognize and respect" those imitations of hers. And here's Mr. Male Dodo-bird, also no stranger to my office today: "The life partner I love most will recognize and respect my"–

Disbelieving what SHE *sees, and horrified at what it portends.*

Oh, no! No, no, no! Tell me "No," God!

In complete shock, SHE *sits and puts down the microphone.*

Heaven forfend, as the religiosos say! It's not "imitations" he wrote. It's – "limitations!" His life partner must recognize and respect his limitations! How could Miss Julie have messed that up! Because she was exhausted, that's why! Because she was working all night, that's why! Because King Kong did teach this schnook penmanship, that's why! "Imitations, limitations". *Mala suerte,* as my Latino friends say!

Well, we'll have to do a little more mischief here, or we'll be tap-dancing around this all night!

Biting off a lower corner of the Love Lists.

There! A computer glitch, you see, has mangled the responses to question #14!

Calling to the offstage JUANITO.

Juanito baby! Come get the Love Lists. Give our willing lambs 15 minutes together before we lead them to erotic slaughter!

Clicking on the microphone, SHE *turns and addresses the singles.*

Computer Pair-Ups, *Va bene,* as my Italian friends say. Onward and upward, hopes high, banners unfurled!

Clicking off the microphone, SHE *turns and addresses the audience.*

You'd better fasten your seat belts! It is going to be a bumpy night!

THE CURTAINS PART.

The lights come up on the corner table. MITCHELL, *wearing a party hat, sits at the table, and fidgets nervously.*

Now ESTRELLA, *also in party hat, comes behind* MITCHELL *and covers his eyes.*

ESTRELLA: *(Imitating KATHARINE HEPBURN)* "The calla lilies are in bloom again, such a strange flower, so guess who's coming to dinner!"

MITCHELL: What? Who is this?

ESTRELLA: *(Imitating GLORIA SWANSON)* "We didn't need words, we had faces. All right, Mr. DeMille, he's ready for his close-up!"

Playfully pulling off his hat, SHE *is shocked at* MITCHELL'S *bald head.*

Oh! Oh! You have no hair!

MITCHELL: *(Putting his hat back on)* Miss, whoever you are, please! My Pair-Up is due any minute. Do we want jealous carnage?

ESTRELLA: *(Sitting)* Jealous carnage! Jealous carnage? Mister, your hair is gone!

MITCHELL: You can't sit here. My Pair-Up is—

ESTRELLA: Ta-dah!

MITCHELL: You?

ESTRELLA: Well, I'm not ecstatic, either. I mean, when I passed you in the lounge last night, I saw thick, full waves. Where are they now – in your stateroom?

MITCHELL: Yes, they are! I opted for honesty tonight. Do you mind?

ESTRELLA: Yes, I do mind! No, I don't. That is, we're supposed to get acquainted, Mr.–

Reading from a nameplate.

Mr. Mitchell Bernard Wykoff.

Holding up her own nameplate.

Estrella Morrison. So? What did happen to your hair? Yanked out in "jealous carnage," whatever that is?

MITCHELL: "Carnage" is today's word.

ESTRELLA: Today's word?

MITCHELL: I increase my vocabulary with a new word every day.

ESTRELLA: Isn't that interesting! The hair, please.

MITCHELL: One day…one day…it flew out the window. I bought a hairpiece which I wish would also fly out the window.

A guarded laugh, meeting with no response.

I may as well confess: I'm not a funny person.

ESTRELLA: You could have fooled me!

MITCHELL: So, where are the glasses?

ESTRELLA: What?

MITCHELL: I've seen you, too, and you wear–

ESTRELLA: *(Pointing to each eye in turn)* Contacts. They're new. I'll tell you something: they hurt. Still – I'm told I look like Jane Fonda in them.

Posing

Your frank opinion. Miss Fonda, is it not?

MITCHELL: I don't think you want my frank opinion, frankly.

ESTRELLA: My! Aren't we off to a fine start!

MITCHELL: *(Beat)* I want to confess something else: Mitchell Bernard Wykoff is not my real name.

ESTRELLA: It's not?

MITCHELL: No. It's not.

ESTRELLA: Dare I ask?

MITCHELL: It's Bernard Mitchell Wykoff.

ESTRELLA: Aha! You have cleverly and fiendishly switched first names!

MITCHELL: Shall I tell you why?

ESTRELLA: Oh, if you only would!

MITCHELL: The initials. It's those initials: BMW. I don't want people mistakenly thinking I'm flashy or pretentious or devil-may-care, like the car.

ESTRELLA: I doubt that many people would find you flashy or pretentious or devil-may-care, Mitchell.

MITCHELL: Thank you. A car, after all, will stamp a person. Ask me how I know this.

ESTRELLA: I can't wait!

MITCHELL: I am senior accountant for the 4th largest car rental firm east of the Mississippi.

ESTRELLA: Isn't that interesting!

MITCHELL: Thank you. Ergo, the name change. "Ergo" means "therefore."

ESTRELLA: Yesterday's word?

MITCHELL: Tomorrow's. I try to keep ahead.

ESTRELLA: Isn't that also interesting! Well, since it's true confessions time, Mitchell, Estrella isn't my real name, either.

MITCHELL: It isn't?

ESTRELLA: It's really "Estelle." But "Estelle" is sort of...sort of–

MITCHELL: Sort of Chevrolet?

ESTRELLA: Yes. Sort of Chevrolet. Don't you find "Estrella" more... more–

MITCHELL: Lexus?

ESTRELLA: You do know how to nail things, don't you, Mitchell!

MITCHELL: Yes, I do.

Beat

Look here, Estrella, this morning, when you were–

ESTRELLA: When I was–?

MITCHELL: You were playing shuffleboard with seven, no eight, no seven other girls–

ESTRELLA: You counted?

MITCHELL: I counted. Anyway, the eight of you–

ESTRELLA: Accounts Receivable.

MITCHELL: I beg your pardon?

ESTRELLA: The whole Accounts Receivable Department came on this cruise together.

MITCHELL: Oh. Well, I saw you and I thought, "Wouldn't it be nice if she's my Pair-Up?" Only–

ESTRELLA: Only?

MITCHELL: Only you had glasses on. I liked you in glasses.

ESTRELLA: You did?

MITCHELL: You looked so...so – serious. Jet black shell with silvertone trim.

ESTRELLA: What?

MITCHELL: Jet black shell with–

ESTRELLA: Car colors?

MITCHELL: I can name 27 of them, alphabetically.

ESTRELLA: You take a girl's breath away, Mitchell!

MITCHELL: Thank you.

A long, awkward beat.

Maybe you've already surmised: I'm an introvert.

ESTRELLA: Who would ever surmise that!

MITCHELL: And too analytical. And overly proper in public places.

ESTRELLA: No!

MITCHELL: Yes. Also, I've been told – boring.

ESTRELLA: It isn't possible!

MITCHELL: Anal-retentive, as well.

ESTRELLA: Perhaps that's more information than I need right now, Mitchell.

MITCHELL: And you?

ESTRELLA: Me? I'm just sort of–

Imitating DIANE KEATON.

"La-di-da. La-di-da. Lobster under the fridge, but la-di-da."

MITCHELL: I beg your pardon?

ESTRELLA: Don't tell me you don't recognize it. "La-di-da" is one of my best, one of my very best!

MITCHELL: Your very best what?

ESTRELLA: It's Diane Keaton, for God's sake! It's *Annie Hall*, for God's sake!

MITCHELL: I beg your pardon?

ESTRELLA: Please! Stop begging my pardon all over the place! I had another of my best ready, I want you to know. But that was when I thought there was hair under the hat. It wouldn't work now.

MITCHELL: I beg your pardon – I mean, what wouldn't work now?

ESTRELLA: Another of my best! See. I thought you had that head of wavy, reddish hair, and I–

MITCHELL: Not reddish, sandalwood.

ESTRELLA: A car color, am I right?

MITCHELL: Right.

ESTRELLA: Since it's all gone, it doesn't really matter, does it! Anyway, you approach with your car-colored hair, and I'd put out my arm to stop you, and I'd say – are you ready? – I'd say:

Imitating BARBRA STREISAND.

"Hello, Gorgeous!" How's that?

MITCHELL: How's what?

ESTRELLA: *(Imitating BARBRA STREISAND again)* "Hello, Gorgeous!" I'd say, "Hello, Gorgeous!"

MITCHELL: I beg your par – I mean, what is it you're driving at?

ESTRELLA: I'm driving at Barbra Streisand, that's what I'm driving at! I'm driving at she said it in the movie and she said it again when she won the Academy Award. "Hello, Gorgeous!" What? It wasn't good? You want a different one?

MITCHELL: A different what?

ESTRELLA: Excuse me a moment.

SHE *gets up from her table and proceeds to Miss Julie's table.*

THE LIGHTS GO DOWN ON MITCHELL.

ESTRELLA: Miss Julie?

MISS JULIE: *(Wanting nothing more than to hide)* Estrella, baby! Your new friend: what do you think?

ESTRELLA: New friend! What new friend? He's the enemy!

MISS JULIE: But that simply cannot be. The Crystal Harmony Cruises Computer Pair-Up always finds–

ESTRELLA: Not this time! This time, the Crystal Harmony Cruises Computer Pair-Up has found a zombie! A hairless one!

MISS JULIE: Estrella, darling! A zombie? Oh, Mitchell Bernard is a bit on the stiff side, perhaps, but certainly not a–

ESTRELLA: Mitchell Bernard isn't even Mitchell Bernard. Mitchell Bernard is Bernard Mitchell! I'm surprised I remember the name: one look at the shiny skull and I lost consciousness!

MISS JULIE: Estrella, Estrella baby! He sometimes wears a small, non-intrusive enhancement, I grant you, but many of our less confident guests do. It's a man thing, the poor dears. Besides, you don't strike me as a girl who would worry about so trifling a thing.

ESTRELLA: I wouldn't. I wouldn't, only–

MISS JULIE: Only?

ESTRELLA: Only I always wanted to push a guy's hair aside on his forehead, like Katie and Hubbell.

MISS JULIE: Katie? Hubbell?

ESTRELLA: Barbra Streisand and Robert Redford.

MISS JULIE: Oh. *The Way It Was*?

ESTRELLA: *The Way We Were.*

MISS JULIE: Sorry.

ESTRELLA: Not that it would matter. Not that he would know what I was up to! Miss Julie, I have told you and told you what I need in a partner, haven't I? Haven't I?

MISS JULIE: *Ad nauseam*, dear. I mean – *ad infinitem*, dear.

ESTRELLA: Have I ever said I needed someone who liked my glasses? Have I?

MISS JULIE: It's the only thing you haven't said, I admit.

ESTRELLA: I spend $300 on contact lenses – itchy, scratchy, burning things! – and he prefers glasses. Nobody prefers glasses. Then, there's the other thing, of course.

MISS JULIE: Other thing?

ESTRELLA: He worries his initials will spell out a car. And if I don't stop him, he'll count 27 car colors in alphabetical order on his fingers! To say nothing of that other thing.

MISS JULIE: My! So many other things!

ESTRELLA: He trots out a new word every two and a half minutes!

MISS JULIE: But surely you admire a person so intent on improving himself! What Mitchell Bernard–

ESTRELLA: Bernard Mitchell.

MISS JULIE: What Bernard Mitchell tries to do is impress with his unique brand of intelligence the special girl who has come into his life.

ESTRELLA: To say nothing about the biggest thing of all!

MISS JULIE: What biggest thing of all is that, Estrella dear?

ESTRELLA: You know what thing is that! The "Biggie!"

MISS JULIE: Oh, that biggest thing!

ESTRELLA: I've done four of my best, four of my all-time best imitations, and what do I get? A blank stare. Four blank stares!

MISS JULIE: *(Tap-dancing, as she knows she must)* I'm sure you misread, Estrella dear.

ESTRELLA: Has he done any imitations? He has not! So – where's the match? That's why we're sitting together in the first place, right? So–

MISS JULIE: Estrella, Estrella, I understand your puzzlement, but I appreciate his reticence, too. I ask you to appreciate it. You're so good at your imitations – no, you are! – and Mitchell sees how good you are and backs off.

ESTRELLA: That isn't it.

MISS JULIE: Oh, but it is! Look at it his way. Before his very eyes, so much talent, an explosion of cleverness, of versatility, in the very first few minutes of the meeting!

ESTRELLA: Yes, but–

MISS JULIE: Think, think! Four of your all-time best imitations in less than – what? Ten minutes? Why, it's overwhelming! That's it, Estrella – you overwhelm!

ESTRELLA: *(A hesitant beat)* You think that's–

MISS JULIE: I know!

ESTRELLA: You really think that's–?

MISS JULIE: You go out there, Miss Estrella Morrison, and focus on the other items on the Love Lists. You'll be awestruck, yes, awestruck, by the Pair-Up you have been dealt.

ESTRELLA: I will?

MISS JULIE: You will! I guarantee it! Then, once he's more comfortable, more accustomed to the dazzle of it all, he'll bend, he'll thaw, he'll join you in your antic gift.

ESTRELLA: He will?

MISS JULIE: He will! Why not review together the question about – oh, favorite authors, perhaps. In the names you have both chosen, there is a match, Estrella, a match made in heaven!

ESTRELLA: There is?

MISS JULIE: There most certainly is. Then, soon, why, you'll just sort of – slide into The "Biggie."

ESTRELLA: But–

MISS JULIE: Trust, Estrella, a soupcon of trust! You're at table with a man in possession of all the "recognizing and respecting" you can use. Claim him, Estrella – oh, claim him, do!

ESTRELLA: But–

MISS JULIE: He's the one, Estrella baby, the one! Would I lie! Would I lie?

ESTRELLA, *more steamrolled than convinced, is pushed back in the direction of her table.*

To the audience.

This job looks like a breeze, right? Hah! Vacuum cleaner salesmen don't work so hard!

Beat

Listen, a secret, okay? I had absolutely no hope for the girl, none, nil, zilch! I mean, let's face it: a raving beauty she's not, Miss Accounts Receivable from Staten Island, no strong selling points here, you see the picture? It gets worse, friends! During the first interview, I nearly fell asleep listening to her story. At age 8, she wins a school talent contest with her Julie Andrews imitation.

SHE *makes a face of disgust.*

"My Favorite Things." Yes! You're glad you weren't present for that one, am I right? Later, she tells me, she gets hooked on old movies. With her first paycheck, she treats herself to Turner Classic Movies. Yes! 24 hours a day! I kid you not! "Get a life, kid!" is what I want to say. Do I? I do not.

Calling out to MITCHELL.

Hairy or not, Mitchell baby, Miss Julie is counting on you! Move in, Mr. Hunk, move in!

Calling out to offstage JUANITO.

Juanito, baby! *Por favor!* Miss Julie has earned a steak, a big juicy steak, two pounds at least. You hear me? And tell them not to stint on *los on-yon-es!*

> THE LIGHTS COME UP ON THE CORNER TABLE
> AS ESTRELLA REACHES IT.

ESTRELLA: I wasn't gone very long, was I, Bernard Mitchell? I mean, Mitchell Bernard?

MITCHELL: Seven minutes, fourteen seconds.

ESTRELLA: You counted?

MITCHELL: *(HE holds up his watch)* Precise to the millisecond.

ESTRELLA: Who'd want a watch that wasn't, I ask myself!

MITCHELL: In your absence, a man brought our Love Lists to the table. Remarkable!

ESTRELLA: What's remarkable?

MITCHELL: How they match. Right off the bat, the computer seems to have chewed them up in exactly the same corner. See?

HE *holds up the Love Lists.*

ESTRELLA: Those look like teeth marks. They can't be teeth marks, can they?

MITCHELL: But the answers, Estrella! Our answers!

ESTRELLA: Yes?

MITCHELL: Breathtaking! Although– ?

ESTRELLA: Although?

MITCHELL: I am surprised Miss Julie could even read mine. My handwriting is terrible. That's one of them, you know.

ESTRELLA: One of them? One of what?

MITCHELL: One of them. You know, one of them.

ESTRELLA: *(Not getting it)* Oh. One of them.

MITCHELL: No matter, look at question #4: "The three authors I love most are–" Third best, Estrella names–

ESTRELLA: Charles Dickens, of course.

MITCHELL: As does Mitchell Bernard, of course.

ESTRELLA: No!

MITCHELL: Yes! Perfect match! While in the #2 spot, Estrella picks–

ESTRELLA: Leo Tolstoy, of course.

MITCHELL: As does Mitchell Bernard! Did you ever?

Jubilantly

And the all-time *Numero Uno* choice of both Estrella and Mitchell Bernard is–

ESTRELLA: No!

MITCHELL: Yes!

ESTRELLA: Danielle Steel?

MITCHELL: Danielle Steel!

ESTRELLA: You can't mean it.

MITCHELL: I do!

ESTRELLA: Isn't that something! I mean, that is something!

MITCHELL: It most certainly is. It most certainly is something. Although–

ESTRELLA: Although–

MITCHELL: I have a confession to make.

ESTRELLA: Another confession?

MITCHELL: Those authors?

ESTRELLA: What about them?

MITCHELL: I'm afraid I haven't really read–

ESTRELLA: You lied?

MITCHELL: Not exactly.

ESTRELLA: You lied about Charles Dickens, Mitchell?

MITCHELL: I've only read one of his books, and not all the way through. *A Christmas Carol*.

ESTRELLA: But, Mitchell – I've only read *A Christmas Carol*, too.

MITCHELL: *(Laughing)* No!

ESTRELLA: *(Laughing)* Yes! And not all the way through!

MITCHELL: Then…then – you never read Leo Tolstoy either?

ESTRELLA *shakes her head.*

And you listed him because–?

ESTRELLA: I listed him because I wanted to sound more…more–

MITCHELL: Intellectual?

ESTRELLA: How did you guess?

MITCHELL: That's why I listed him.

ESTRELLA: You didn't!

MITCHELL: I did!

ESTRELLA: It's incredible!

MITCHELL: Oh, it's incredible, all right. It is most definitely incredible!

ESTRELLA: You know what we are? We are two of a kind!

MITCHELL: Two sides of a coin!

ESTRELLA: Two peas in a pod!

MITCHELL & ESTRELLA: Two bugs in a rug!

MITCHELL: *(Laughing)* Furthermore–

ESTRELLA: Furthermore?

MITCHELL: *(Laughing)* I lied about Danielle Steel, too!

ESTRELLA: *(Crestfallen)* Oh, Mitchell! You didn't!

MITCHELL: What's wrong?

ESTRELLA: I have read all of Danielle Steel's books. Twice!

MITCHELL: I am sorry.

ESTRELLA: But why, Mitchell, why would you lie about–

MITCHELL: I wanted to be part of the…of the – popular taste. It's another one of my – you know.

ESTRELLA: Your what?

MITCHELL: You know.

ESTRELLA: I don't.

MITCHELL: My limitations.

ESTRELLA: Your–! Why are we speaking of anything so depressing as limitations?

Covering her ears.

No. I won't listen! You're spoiling things!

MITCHELL: Am I spoiling things?

ESTRELLA: Yes! You are!

Brightening

Still…maybe it's not irreparable. I mean, after all, if you've never read Danielle Steel's books, and I've read them twice, that evens things out, doesn't it? I mean–

Imitating BETTE DAVIS.

"Let's not ask for the moon, Jerry. We have the stars."

MITCHELL: What?

ESTRELLA: I said–

Imitating BETTE DAVIS again.

"Let's not ask for the moon, Jerry. We have the–"

MITCHELL: But my name is Mitchell.

ESTRELLA: I know it's Mitchell, Mitchell. But Bette Davis didn't say, "Let's not ask for the moon, Mitchell." She said – oh, never mind. It's my fault. I thought I could get away with just one little one.

MITCHELL: One little what?

ESTRELLA: One little tearful, but hopeful, *Now, Voyager* moment. It doesn't really overwhelm, does it? Or does it?

Crying out.

Yes, it does! Bette Davis and I: the combination is overwhelming!

SHE *covers her face with her hands.*

MITCHELL: Excuse me a second.

HE *gets up from his table and proceeds to Miss Julie's table.*

THE LIGHTS GO DOWN ON ESTRELLA.

MITCHELL: Miss Julie?

MISS JULIE: *(Nearly choking on her steak)* Why, how nice, Mitchell! I mean Bernard. I mean Mitchell. How's it going?

MITCHELL: It is not going. It is not going at all. It won't work!

MISS JULIE: Of course, it will work. The Crystal Harmony Computer Pair-Up always works. The Love Lists always–

MITCHELL: There is something wrong with that girl.

MISS JULIE: With our Estrella? No!

MITCHELL: Something terribly, terribly wrong.

MISS JULIE: Never!

MITCHELL: She's on some kind of crazy happy juice! She's not there! She is somewhere else!

MISS JULIE: *(Starting to tap-dance again)* Oh, but which of us isn't, Mitchell?

MITCHELL: I thought I wanted to know her. Now that I know her, I'm not sure I want to know her.

MISS JULIE: I'm afraid I'm not following.

MITCHELL: Why isn't she wearing her glasses? The girl on the deck was–

MISS JULIE: Was–?

MITCHELL: The other girls in the game were laughing and cheering and clowning and…and then there was this one girl, standing slightly apart from them, looking – I don't know – a little bit sad, a little bit lonely. And serious, very serious. And I thought, "This girl might listen to me, might care about me, no matter what my shortcomings are. This girl," I thought, "this is a quiet girl, who doesn't care about designer glasses, with turquoise and sequins, no, someone who would understand that I do the best I can with what I have to offer her."

MISS JULIE: You got all that from her glasses?

MITCHELL: They were jet black shell with silvertone trim.

MISS JULIE: But Mitchell – those sound like car colors.

MITCHELL: Exactly.

MISS JULIE: Oh, but she's got on those itchy, burning contacts for you, Mitchell, because she wants to look her prettiest.

MITCHELL: It doesn't matter now. There's that other thing.

MISS JULIE: *(All innocence)* What other thing, Mitchell?

MITCHELL: "La-di-da, la-di-da!"

MISS JULIE: Oh. That other thing.

MITCHELL: Serious? Her? She's dizzy, ditzy and dizzy! "La-di-da –" what is that?

MISS JULIE: *(Really winging it by now)* It's a tic, Mitchell, just a harmless little tic. She's a bit insecure, that's all. Many of our Crystal Harmony girls are insecure, you know. It's a female thing, the poor dears. Have you forgotten your own little deception?

SHE *points to his head.*

Oh, I grant you, she may overdo it just a little–

MITCHELL: A little!

MISS JULIE: A lot? But pretending to be someone else, some character in a movie, perhaps, is an indication to me that she worries she may not pleasure you. And, Mitchell, you don't strike me as a man who would let a girl's fragilities get in the way of–

MITCHELL: And what about the other thing, please?

MISS JULIE: What other thing?

MITCHELL: "The Biggie!" My "Biggie!"

MISS JULIE: Oh. That other thing.

MITCHELL: Will she let me talk about them? Absolutely not!

MISS JULIE: About–?

MITCHELL: My limitations!

MISS JULIE: Oh. Those.

MITCHELL: How can she recognize and respect them when she won't even listen to them?

MISS JULIE: *(The tap-dance supreme)* But it's so easily explained! She wants you to feel warm, comforted, joyously present in her joyous presence first!

MITCHELL: What???

MISS JULIE: Yes! She wants you to sense her essential inward compassion, revealing itself in her essential outward effusion!

MITCHELL: What???

MISS JULIE: Yes! I make this suggestion to you, Mitchell. If you sort of – sidle into your limitations, lean into them softly, gently, as the evening progresses, if you deal with the other items on the Love Lists–

MITCHELL: But–

MISS JULIE: No buts, no buts, not a single but! Estrella awaits. Go back to your table this instant. Glow in the great match you share. And glow you will, Mitchell, glow you will!

MITCHELL: I will?

MISS JULIE: You will! In a little while, you'll see, she'll be much more relaxed with you. Why, you will slide right into your "Biggie!"

MITCHELL: I will?

MISS JULIE: You will! For now, why not try the question about – oh, about the foods you love. Her eyes will sparkle in perfect compatibility.

MITCHELL: They will?

MISS JULIE: Framed like Christmas candles in the window!

MITCHELL: I'd rather see them framed in jet black shell with silvertone trim.

MISS JULIE: Whatever! She's the one, baby, she's the one! Would I lie? Would I lie?

Assuaged, MITCHELL *leaves and heads back to his table.*

Exhausted, MISS JULIE *falls into her chair and faces the audience.*

A match made in heaven? No match is made in heaven! They're made right here, at Miss Julie's table. And Miss Julie knows that those two were put on this planet for each other. Listen, a secret, okay? When I met Mr. Dodo-bird, I said to myself, "All is lost. Unemployment perdition lies ahead!" I mean, Mitchell Bernard, or Bernard Mitchell, whatever his name is, leans over and whispers to me – get this! "My girlfriend of three months has broken off with me because she thinks I'm boring." It took her three months to figure that one out? Well, duh!

Calling out to the corner table.

Estrella baby, Mitchell baby: there is a lot riding on you. I have this small bet with Juanito: those 100 *pesos* he has owed me for a century now? Cancelled, gone, forgotten if – if you connect! Yes! I don't ask you to come through for me, guys, but for Juanito!

To the audience.

Miss Julie has a heart as big as this ship, you know. But you have already figured that out, right?

THE LIGHTS GO DOWN.

They come up again at the corner table as MITCHELL *approaches it.*

MITCHELL: I'm sorry I was gone so long.

ESTRELLA: It's okay, Mitchell. I'm sorry I overwhelmed you. In your absence, I've looked at the Love Lists again and it's quite remarkable, really! Our responses–

MITCHELL: Absolutely coincide!

ESTRELLA: Yes! Question #5, for example: "The three foods I love most are–"

MITCHELL: Match?

ESTRELLA: Perfect! Ergo – note the word – I ordered for us.

MITCHELL: You what?

ESTRELLA: While you were gone, the waiter came by and–

MITCHELL: It's the man's job to order, Estrella.

ESTRELLA: Doris Day ordered for her man. Audrey Hepburn ordered for her man. Didn't you know that?

MITCHELL: No. I did not.

ESTRELLA: Well, since I know how hungry you senior accountants can get, and I also know exactly what three foods you like best, I–

MITCHELL: Estrella, if a man lists three favorite foods, that doesn't mean he wants all three at the same meal.

ESTRELLA: Silly person! I did not order all three!

MITCHELL: Well, that's good.

ESTRELLA: I ordered two.

MITCHELL: Two?

ESTRELLA: The first course for Estrella and Mitchell will be–

MITCHELL: Pasta?

ESTRELLA: Pasta for two coming up! Not just pasta, but pasta with red sauce and–

MITCHELL: Basil? No!

ESTRELLA: Yes! What I wrote, exactly as I wrote it!

MITCHELL: No!

ESTRELLA: And the second course for Estrella and Mitchell will be–?

MITCHELL: Wild salmon?

ESTRELLA: Wild salmon for two coming up! With cashews, of course.

MITCHELL: What?

ESTRELLA: With cashews, of course.

MITCHELL: I never wrote "with cashews, of course."

ESTRELLA: That's a given, Mitchell: wild salmon comes with cashews.

MITCHELL: Cashews are far from a given! I hate cashews!

ESTRELLA: Oh! I am sorry. If I sort of push them to the side of your plate for you? Will that do?

Covering her face, about to cry.

I can see that it won't.

MITCHELL: Don't cry again, Estrella. It's a very thoughtful gesture you propose.

ESTRELLA: I do try to be thoughtful.

MITCHELL: And so you are. I'll push the cashews to the side of my plate. How's that?

ESTRELLA: You will? It's all fixed then, isn't it!

Brightening

I was just a bit puzzled by what to do about your #3 favorite – and mine, I hasten to add – and then I thought, "Why not?" I thought, "Why not take the mad gamble and propose that Estrella and Mitchell lunch tomorrow?"

MITCHELL: Lunch tomorrow? Why not?

ESTRELLA: Wonderful! Lunch tomorrow will be–

Pointing to MITCHELL's *Love List.*

For Mitchell Bernard Wykoff, his #3 favorite: chicken salad on whole wheat toast, tomato on the side.

Pointing to her own Love List.

For Estrella Morrison, her #3 favorite: chicken salad on whole wheat toast, guess what on the side?

MITCHELL: No!

ESTRELLA: Yes!

MITCHELL: Isn't that something!

ESTRELLA: It is! It most definitely is something!

MITCHELL: It's – uncanny! Wednesday's word.

ESTRELLA: Oh, it's uncanny, all right. It is most definitely uncanny!

MITCHELL: You know what we are? We are two for the road!

ESTRELLA: And two on the nose!

MITCHELL: And two kernels on the cob!

MITCHELL & ESTRELLA: And two is company!

ESTRELLA: Oh, Mitchell! We agree so totally on things. We are so thoughtful, pushing cashews aside and all, I feel comfortable about asking a little favor. At lunch tomorrow–?

MITCHELL: At lunch tomorrow?

ESTRELLA: When the chicken salad sandwiches arrive? Could we – that is, could you – do the scene with our server?

MITCHELL: The scene?

ESTRELLA: The scene! I've always wanted to be part of the scene!

MITCHELL: Part of what scene?

ESTRELLA: You know! The sandwiches arrive. You look straight at the server. You say – oh, I know I don't do this well – you say...

Imitating JACK NICHOLSON.

"Now all you have to do is hold the chicken, bring me the toast, give me a check for the chicken salad sandwich, and you haven't broken any rules."

Bursting with laughter.

You can add, if you want, "Between your knees."

MITCHELL: I beg your pardon?

ESTRELLA: "Hold the chicken between your knees." I've seen comics do it that way.

MITCHELL: Do what what way?

ESTRELLA: Oh, yes, Mitchell! I've heard them!

Imitating JACK NICHOLSON again.

"Hold the chicken between your knees."

MITCHELL: That's disgusting!

ESTRELLA: No! It's funny!

Aware he doesn't get the joke.

Jack Nicholson. *Five Easy Pieces.*

MITCHELL: Five easy what?

ESTRELLA: *Five Easy Pieces.* Oh, my Jack Nicholson isn't good, I know, seeing I'm a woman and all. But your Jack Nicholson? Your Jack Nicholson must be great!

MITCHELL: My what must be great?

ESTRELLA: You're kidding, right? In this diner, the snippy waitress says, "No side orders," and Jack Nicholson looks straight at her and sneers–

MITCHELL: "Hold the chicken between your legs?"

ESTRELLA: Not the legs, the knees! Between her knees! And you don't even have to add that part. Please, Mitchell? You don't mind my asking?

MITCHELL: *(Standing, a bit angry)* I am chagrined, Estrella, absolutely chagrined!

ESTRELLA: *(Standing, a bit angry herself)* That must be Monday's word!

MITCHELL: Sunday's. "Do the scene?" I will do no such thing!

ESTRELLA: You won't?

MITCHELL: "Hold the chicken between your knees?" I will say no such thing!

ESTRELLA: Not even for me?

MITCHELL: Not even for anybody!

ESTRELLA: Excuse me a moment.

ESTRELLA *gets up from her table and proceeds to Miss Julie's table.*

THE LIGHTS GO DOWN ON MITCHELL.

ESTRELLA: Listen up, Miss Julie, baby!

MISS JULIE: *(Spritzing the water she's just drunk)* Why, Estrella, what a nice surprise! And how are things?

ESTRELLA: And how are things? And how are things? I'll tell you how are things! Things are in the toilet, that's how are things!

MISS JULIE: But surely that cannot be, Estrella.

ESTRELLA: I am sitting across from the prize-winning nerd on this boat!

MISS JULIE: This is not a boat, dear: this is a ship.

ESTRELLA: You want proof? I have proof! He eats his wild salmon without cashews!

MISS JULIE: Is that all! Lots of people eat their wild salmon without–

ESTRELLA: You want more proof? He counts things! He counts everything!

MISS JULIE: But surely–

ESTRELLA: I'm telling you, everything!   Milliseconds!   Accounts Receivable girls! Everything! I'll bet that right now, he's decided to count cashews.

MISS JULIE: I hardly think–

ESTRELLA: Yes, I'm sure of it! First he'll count the cashews on his plate. Then, he'll count the cashews on my plate. You know, of course, he's anal-retentive.

MISS JULIE: Why would you even think that, Estrella?

ESTRELLA: I don't think it. I know it! He announced it!

MISS JULIE: I see. Still, Estrella, lots of people, good people, sensitive people are anal-retentive. It can be a positive thing, a real plus!

ESTRELLA: What???

MISS JULIE: Yes! Anal-retentives remember things, you know, things like birthdays and anniversaries and where we have misplaced our car keys. That can be very comforting to a girl. Think of Mitchell as a human Rolodex!

ESTRELLA: *(Looking wistfully toward* MITCHELL*)* And I had such hopes. I thought, "This guy needs someone, someone like me to loosen him up, to" – but no! No, no, no!

MISS JULIE: You're fighting a very touching sentiment there, my girl!

ESTRELLA: I thought, "This guy has a gentle–"

MISS JULIE: A gentle doofus-ness?

ESTRELLA: Yes, a gentle – but no! No, no, no!

MISS JULIE: All told, an "okay guy," perhaps?

ESTRELLA: Well, yes, but – no! No, no, no! There's no getting around the important thing, after all.

MISS JULIE: What important thing is that, dear?

ESTRELLA: You know what important thing!

MISS JULIE: Oh. That important thing.

ESTRELLA: Yes, the "Biggie!" Does he recognize my imitations? He does not! Does he respect them? He does not. Will he do Jack Nicholson? He will not. My God, everybody does Jack Nicholson!

MISS JULIE: Shall I tell you what I think, sweet girl? I think that he's reluctant to do his imitations for the simple reason that he dislikes public display. I'm sure that in private–

ESTRELLA: Hah!

MISS JULIE: No, I mean this! I do! He's shy about going over the top in front of all those Crystal Harmony nighttime revelers.

ESTRELLA: I did not ask him to do Jack Nicholson in front of any nighttime revelers. I asked him to do Jack Nicholson at lunch! There are no nighttime revelers at lunch, are there?

Breaking down in tears.

Such a small thing to ask, such a simple request!

MISS JULIE: Tears, Estrella, so many tears! "Why?" I ask myself in my heart of hearts. Years of experience tell me that you see depths in our Mitchell, depths you would like to discover, to explore. You need more time with the man, more time to find beneath the skin of a senior accountant the soul of a gypsy.

ESTRELLA: Beneath the skin of that senior accountant is the soul of a senior accountant!

MISS JULIE: So hard, so very hard, my Estrella. Why, I recall how he answered question #7 on his Love List, his "favorite dances," his obvious affinity for all those wild, passionate, Latin rhythms.

ESTRELLA: Latin rhythms! Forget it! A stiff like him doesn't dance! He doesn't do anything, he doesn't like anything! Except car colors!

MISS JULIE: But–

ESTRELLA: No! I'm going back to my room and re-read Danielle Steel's *No Greater Love*!

SHE *starts off.*

MISS JULIE: *(It's last-ditch time)* If you're so determined, I'll tell you what I shall do, my dear girl. You go out there and spend twenty more minutes with him, just twenty. If things don't change for the better, Miss Julie will match you with someone else tomorrow night.

ESTRELLA: Someone who doesn't count things?

MISS JULIE: Someone who doesn't count things.

ESTRELLA: Someone who doesn't name car colors?

MISS JULIE: Ditto.

ESTRELLA: Someone who knows that cashews belong with salmon?

MISS JULIE: Ditto again.

ESTRELLA: Someone who will recognize and respect my–

MISS JULIE: That's the tough part of the order! But I will try. And, Miss Julie will eat the extra charge for computer time.

ESTRELLA: You're not just saying twenty minutes, when you mean twenty-one minutes?

MISS JULIE: Would I lie? Would I lie?

ESTRELLA: All right! Twenty minutes! By his watch: it's precise to the millisecond.

SHE *heads back to her table.*

MISS JULIE: *(To the audience)* And I thought being assistant manager of sheets-and-towels at Fortunoff's was a tough racket! That was easy!

Beat

Listen, a secret, okay? When I saw the Love Lists, "recognize and respect my blah-blah?" "Miss Julie," I said to myself, "you are saved! Here is manna from heaven! Miss Estrella Nothing-Much and Mr. Mitchell Bernard Nothing-At-All are so thoroughly matched that Miss Julie is saved!" And now, one letter! One cockamamie letter!!! Are we now to allow one letter, not even a major letter, but a measly 'l' buried in the middle of the alphabet, to throw it all off? The gods must be crazy!

Toward the corner table.

Hop to it, you two!

Calling to offstage JUANITO.

Juanito! Miss Julie needs a margarita, pronto! Make it a double, *amigo*, because the gods are as crazy as bedbugs tonight!

SHE *fetches a three-panel screen and puts it around her for privacy.*

Excuse, please.

THE LIGHTS COME UP ON MITCHELL
AS ESTRELLA APPROACHES THE TABLE.

ESTRELLA: I didn't take so long, did I?

Spotting empty dishes on the table.

What's this?

MITCHELL: I sort of got hungry. I sort of ate my dinner.

ESTRELLA: You–?

MITCHELL: I sort of ate my pasta. I was still sort of hungry, so I sort of ate my salmon, too.

ESTRELLA: First, of course, you sort of pushed–?

MITCHELL: Yes. There were seven whole cashews and eleven partial cashews on my plate.

ESTRELLA: You counted!

In MISS JULIE's *direction.*

He counted!

MITCHELL: While on your plate, there were only six whole cashews and four partial cashews.

ESTRELLA: And nineteen minutes to go.

MITCHELL: What?

ESTRELLA: Nothing. I was sort of counting, myself.

MITCHELL: But don't you find it ironic? That I, who dislikes cashews, got more on my plate than you, who likes cashews?

ESTRELLA: Ironic? It's hair-raising, positively hair-raising!

MITCHELL: *(Instinctively grabbing at his scalp)* You're making fun of me.

ESTRELLA: No, Mitchell, no. I didn't mean that kind of hair-raising. I meant that, well – I've known bean counters in my day, and paper-clip counters in my day, but I never met a cashew counter before.

MITCHELL: Then you are making fun of me!

ESTRELLA: No, Mitchell, no. People who count cashews remember birthdays and anniversaries and know where the car keys are, and that's – comforting.

MITCHELL: Thank you. So, anyway, you now have thirteen whole cashews and fifteen partial cashews on your plate.

ESTRELLA: You've checked that none broke during the transfer, then?

Looking at her watch.

Sixteen minutes to go.

MITCHELL: What?

ESTRELLA: Nothing, nothing, Mitchell. I need to ask you something and I need an honest answer, okay? It's about #7 on the Love List, okay? Because, in my experience, people who count cashews and car colors and stuff don't like dancing. So my question to you is–

MITCHELL: But that's so funny! It's just so–

ESTRELLA: So–?

MITCHELL: In your absence, Estrella? I asked the orchestra to play some of our favorites. Yours and mine.

ESTRELLA: Yours and mine? Mine and yours? Favorites?

MITCHELL: Well, of course, favorites.

ESTRELLA: Favorite dances?

MITCHELL: Actually, it is quite remarkable.

ESTRELLA: It is?

MITCHELL: It's more than that. It's almost – inexplicable! A February word.

Reading from the Love Lists.

"The dances I love most are–" Mitchell's response: #3, the waltz.

ESTRELLA: No!

MITCHELL: Yes! Estrella's response–

ESTRELLA: #3 – the waltz!

MITCHELL: Next on the list: Mitchell's response: #2, the tango.

ESTRELLA: No!

MITCHELL: Yes! Estrella's response–

ESTRELLA: #2 – the tango!

MITCHELL: And in the #1 slot? The all-time favorite, *Numero Uno* choice? Mitchell's response–

As the band strikes up a rumba.

I do believe that is my #1 choice they are honoring, Estrella.

ESTRELLA: No!

MITCHELL: Yes! The rumba! Yours, too! The rumba!

ESTRELLA: Oh, Mitchell!

MITCHELL: Uncanny enough for you?

ESTRELLA: Breathtakingly uncanny!

MITCHELL: Beyond coincidence?

ESTRELLA: Breathtakingly beyond coincidence!

MITCHELL: You know what we are? We are two on the aisle!

ESTRELLA: Two to get ready!

MITCHELL: Two for the price of one!

MITCHELL & ESTRELLA: Two who can live as cheaply as–

As one, THEY *put fingers to lips – it is too soon to hint at that.*

Sorry.

ESTRELLA: But, Mitchell – you've no idea how happy this makes me.

MITCHELL: Likewise.

ESTRELLA: So happy I simply cannot resist! I see no reason whatsoever to resist!

SHE *stands and begins to move her hips languorously.*

MITCHELL: Resist what? What is that you're doing?

27

ESTRELLA: (SHE *begins her LAUREN BACALL imitation by whistling*) "You know how to whistle, don't you, Steve?"

MITCHELL: Estrella! Please! My name is not Steve. It's–

ESTRELLA: *(Imitating LAUREN BACALL again)* "You put your lips together and you blow!"

MITCHELL: Please! Stop putting your lips together. You'll draw attention. I can't stand attention!

ESTRELLA: *(Imitating MAE WEST now)* "Mmm – why don't you come up sometime and see me!" You know, Mitchell? A lot of people think that line is "Why don't you come up and see me sometime?" But it's not! It's "Why don't you come up sometime and–"

MITCHELL: Sit, Estrella. You must sit!

ESTRELLA: How can I sit? I'm bursting with joy! And when that happens–

Calling out to nighttime revelers.

Nighttime revelers! Mitchell's favorite dance is the rumba. Estrella's favorite dance is the rumba! Is this a rhythmic paradise or what?

To MITCHELL.

Let's not waste a note, Mitchell. Whirl me into our rhythmic paradise!

MITCHELL: What?

ESTRELLA: Yes! Lead me into rumba heaven–

MITCHELL: What!!!

ESTRELLA: –my hips blending into your hips. One big hip on the polished floor!

MITCHELL: One big–! There's a huge misunderstanding here, Estrella, huge, huge!

ESTRELLA: Tell me later!

MITCHELL: Not later, now! Those dances I named–?

ESTRELLA: *(Gyrating wildly to the music)* Who am I, Mitchell? Imagine fruits on my head, bananas, cherries! Around my neck, rows and rows of beads! On my feet, gold platform shoes! Who am I?

MITCHELL: Estrella, everyone's watching us. I can't stand to have people watching!

ESTRELLA: I love it!

Going into a CARMEN MIRANDA routine.

Think! The Forties! Good neighbors in South America! 20th Century-Fox musicals! Who, Mitchell, who?

MITCHELL: Who what?

ESTRELLA: Think, Mitchell, think!

Doing a CARMEN MIRANDA song.

"Chico, chico, from Puerto Rico

Every muchachita want to go where he go."

MITCHELL: Where who go? I mean, where who goes?

ESTRELLA: You know. You must know.

Continuing the song.

"When he rumba, or bolero,

He do better job than Cesar Romero!"

Now ESTRELLA grabs MITCHELL and dances around with him, trying to engage him in her spirited gyrations. But HE is a stick, lifeless and clumsy.

MITCHELL: STOP!

ESTRELLA: What is wrong? What?

MITCHELL: I have been trying to tell you! Estrella, the dances I named? I watch them. I like to watch them. I don't dance them. I do not dance!

ESTRELLA: Not a – step?

MITCHELL: Not a step.

ESTRELLA: Not a single–?

MITCHELL: I have trouble enough just walking, Estrella.

ESTRELLA: Oh!

MITCHELL: So, please? Sit down? They're starting to stare. I can't stand to have people stare at me!

ESTRELLA cries out in pain and goes to the table. SHE sinks into her chair, her head in her hands.

MITCHELL can take no more. HE runs out, colliding with the three-panel screen that MISS JULIE is putting away.

MISS JULIE: Mitchell! What is the matter?

MITCHELL: I can't bear it!

MISS JULIE: Why, what is it you can't bear, Mitchell, dear?

MITCHELL: Everything! Her! I can't bear her!

MISS JULIE: Estrella? Surely you can't mean our–

MITCHELL: I mean your Estrella, the one with the loopy improvisations!

MISS JULIE: Imitations.

MITCHELL: Whatever they are! They're coming one after the other now, like some faulty assembly line! She's "on" every minute, Miss Julie, every single minute!

MISS JULIE: Oh, but perhaps you think she's "on" every minute because you, my dear Mitchell, are never "on". Dear, dear man, if you could just learn to bend, to thaw, to join her in–

MITCHELL: Join her? Join her!!! You're as nutty as she is!

MISS JULIE: Still waters do run deep, after all. And under that staid exterior of yours, I sense a naughty rascal, with an exuberance that equals our Estrella's!

MITCHELL: No! Not as nutty! You're nuttier! Incrementally so!

MISS JULIE: Today's new word?

MITCHELL: Thursday's. Look: let's get to that other thing, okay?

MISS JULIE: *(All innocence)* What other thing is that?

MITCHELL: You know what other thing.

MISS JULIE: I suppose you mean–?

MITCHELL: Yes! The "Biggie!" Have you forgotten my "Biggie?"

MISS JULIE: I'm glad you bring that up, Mitchell. Indeed, I have not forgotten: "The partner I love most will–"

MITCHELL: "–recognize and respect my limitations."

MISS JULIE: Exactly! But you see, Mitchell, dear, I envision those limitations vanishing, vanishing before our very eyes!

MITCHELL: Whose very eyes?

MISS JULIE: Ours! Poof! If you weren't such a tight-ass, you'd see for yourself.

MITCHELL: I'm not a tight-ass. I'm anal-retentive.

MISS JULIE: You name car colors? You count cashews? Tight-ass!

MITCHELL: Anal-retentive!

MISS JULIE: And so very proper in public places. Tight-ass, if ever I saw it.

MITCHELL: Anal-retentive if ever you saw it!

MISS JULIE: Whatever. My job here, my primary job here, is to point out to you that a "limitation" is merely an "imitation" with an 'l.'

MITCHELL: What???

MISS JULIE: And that, conversely, an "imitation" is merely a "limitation" without an 'l.'

MITCHELL: What???

MISS JULIE: Given the way the world sees these things, an "imitation" is almost a "limitation" just as a "limitation" is an "imitation" in a different light.

MITCHELL: Are you deliberately trying to confuse me?

MISS JULIE: *(The ultimate tap-dance of the night)* Au contraire! Incrementally, to use your excellent word, one letter, one letter alone, separates you from the life partner of your dreams. We must confront that letter!

MITCHELL: *(Holding his head in pain)* I'm getting this terrific headache.

MISS JULIE: Oh, look, Mitchell, look! See what our Estrella is up to now. At this very moment!

MITCHELL: *(Covering his eyes)* I don't want to know!

MISS JULIE: She is removing her contact lenses. Yes! Mitchell! She is scrambling through her purse for–! I can barely believe it! Oh, you owe it to yourself to see this!

MITCHELL: *(Eyes still covered)* No! I won't!

MISS JULIE: She is looking for her glasses, Mitchell! For what reason, you must ask yourself!

MITCHELL: It is obvious.

MISS JULIE: Yes! It is obvious!

MITCHELL: Her contact lenses are itching.

MISS JULIE: No, Mitchell, no! It's an act of love for you! I know an act of love when I see one! Oh, Mitchell, to let a girl like that out of your life! A girl with such flair, such imagination!

MITCHELL: Imagination like hers can make your hair stand on end!

MISS JULIE: But, Mitchell, you have no hair to stand on end. Oh, look, look!

MITCHELL: *(Covering his eyes again)* What's she up to now?

MISS JULIE: She has found her glasses. She is wiping away a tear before she puts them on, a tear that speaks of love and loss. Such glasses, Mitchell. Such serious glasses.

MITCHELL: Jet black shell with–?

MISS JULIE: –silvertone trim!

MITCHELL: Really?

MISS JULIE: Oh, Mitchell, do look at her. No, I mean it, look at her! A girl in serious glasses and yours, yours, if only you can release those devilish recesses you harbor deep, deep within. Oh, Mitchell, she waits so eagerly for the call, that wild roar to tell her her life partner will return to claim the jewel he has been offered. Claim it, Mitchell! Claim her! You have – six minutes to claim her!

MITCHELL: Six?

MISS JULIE: Now five!

MITCHELL: *(Finally uncovering his eyes)* No.

MISS JULIE: Mitchell! Are you forgetting your ex-girlfriend? "Boring," she called you, and let's face it, boring you are! Fight it! Fight! You have – four minutes.

MITCHELL: Four? Why?

MISS JULIE: *(Tap-dancing again)* Uh – no girl will wait alone at a table for more than four minutes. It's a proven fact!

MITCHELL: No.

A few steps away.

How? How can I claim her?

A few steps further away.

No. I won't.

MISS JULIE: Dare I suggest–?

MITCHELL: Suggest?

MISS JULIE: No. I dare not.

MITCHELL: Okay, then.

HE *starts off again.*

MISS JULIE: *(Quickly)* If you could only bring yourself to join her, Mitchell, yes, to join her in her antic gift!

MITCHELL: You don't mean–?

MISS JULIE: I do mean! It's an incrementally great idea. It's the most incrementally great idea ever!

MITCHELL: No.

MISS JULIE: Yes, Mitchell, yes! It can't be so difficult.

MITCHELL: I do not do imitations!

MISS JULIE: But you don't know that – you have never tried. Do one, just one! Look at her, Mitchell! Look at those glasses!

MITCHELL: Jet black shell with–

MISS JULIE: –silvertone trim. Such serious glasses! I have never seen such serious glasses!

MITCHELL: *(Looking at ESTRELLA a long time)* You really think she's put them on for me?

MISS JULIE: Absolutely, positively sure of it!

MITCHELL: No.

HE *takes a few steps and stops.*

No. I cannot.

MISS JULIE: Yes. You can. You can! Only a few minutes worth, Mitchell!

MITCHELL: But…but who would I– ?

MISS JULIE: Anyone. Anyone! Cary Grant. He's an easy one. Do Cary Grant!

MITCHELL: I don't begin to–

MISS JULIE: But you do. You must!

Imitating CARY GRANT.

Judy! Judy! Judy!

MITCHELL: *(Tentatively, weakly, softly, and badly imitating CARY GRANT)* Judy, Judy, Judy. It's impossible.

MISS JULIE: You're not the Cary Grant type, that's all. Try – well, try… Charles Boyer.

MITCHELL: Who?

MISS JULIE: Charles Boyer.

Imitating CHARLES BOYER.

"Come wiz me to the–"

MITCHELL: Oh! I know that one! I do!

Tentatively, weakly, softly and badly imitating CHARLES BOYER.

"Come wiz me to the *Casbah*, my adored one, yes?" Good?

MISS JULIE: No, it wasn't good, Mitchell. You have the makings, I know. I have absolutely, positively no doubt that you have the makings. Only–

MITCHELL: Only?

MISS JULIE: Your anal-retentive heart isn't in it. Look at her, my dear friend, look at her and – preponderate! My word for today, Mitchell!

MITCHELL: Is that really a word?

MISS JULIE: How do I know? You're the one with the vocabulary.

MITCHELL *tries to think, but he is too harried.* HE *starts off.* HE *stops and looks wistfully at* ESTRELLA, *who is rising from the table, about to leave.*

She's leaving, Mitchell, out of your life forever! Do something! Get some anal-retentive blood pumping and DO SOMETHING!

MITCHELL *looks at* ESTRELLA *again and comes to a major decision.* HE *removes his jacket, folding it neatly on a chair.* HE *does the same thing with his shirt and tie until he is down to his undershirt.*

Now, deliberately and purposefully, HE *tears his undershirt to shreds.* HE *raises both hands to his head and exactly like MARLON BRANDO yells out his lusty pain with all his might.*

MITCHELL: *(Imitating MARLON BRANDO)* HEY, ESTRELLA! HEY, ESTRELLA!

ESTRELLA *hears and sees him, and realizing the import of his act, rushes into his arms.* HE *carries her off, kissing her madly.*

THE CURTAINS CLOSE ON THEM.

MISS JULIE: *(Alone on stage, exultant, exhausted)* Bull's eye! Bingo! Hole in one! Triple croquet! Crystal Harmony Cruises and the fabulous Miss Julie have done it again!

Laughing triumphantly, SHE *turns to the audience.*

What did I tell you about the corner table? Was I right? Was I right? You bet your sweet patootie, I was right! There's no real magic in it: either you know your job or you don't.

Laughing again.

Well, maybe a little magic in it. I mean – bad penmanship, imitations, limitations, an extra 'l'. Whatever! Remind me to look up "preponderate" in the dictionary.

Calling to offstage JUANITO.

Juanito! Those hundred *pesos, amigo*? You owe me nothing! Zero, zilch, *nada!*

SHE *takes her coat down from the coat rack.* SHE *looks at the wire hanger in her hand.*

Imitations! What is the fun in them, I wonder.

Looking around to make sure no one is watching, SHE *decides on an imitation of her own, just to test the fun of it.*

SHE *imitates FAYE DUNAWAY imitating JOAN CRAWFORD.*

"NO–WIRE–HANGERS!!!"

SHE *laughs mightily, and, shaking her head, walks offstage.*

THE LIGHTS GO DOWN
END OF PLAY

W. 57, FAB 1 BR, SUNNY STEAL

a one-act play

W. 57, Fab 1 BR, Sunny Steal

production history:

In May 2000, this play was presented by Theatre With Your Coffee in Miami, Florida. It was directed by Jen Ryan with the following cast:

Simone . . . . .Ellen Simmons
Joel . . . . Michael MacEachem
Maddelena . . . . Lisa Boggio

setting:

Interior, an apartment, vacant except for bridge table and chairs.

time:

A fiercely rainy night in October, about 6:30 p.m.

characters:

SIMONE, 55

JOEL, 31

MADDELENA, 27

AT RISE: SIMONE, *seated at the table, talks into her cellular phone.*

SIMONE: *(Into phone)* No, she's not here yet, but I'll tell you the truth, Estelle, I'm glad... Because I did a dumb thing. I left her file at home, would you believe it? It's been that kind of day... No, I called Joel. He'll bring it... I think we are getting along these days, actually... Sort of – who knows with sons? At least I haven't heard any of those speeches lately, "We're entitled to one great hour on earth," blah, blah... Listen, Estelle, take care of that back, and don't move, you hear? I'll handle whatever-her-name-is, don't you worry... Yes, I'll call you. Bye.

SHE *puts down the phone. Now, in thought about* JOEL, *she starts to munch hamburger/French fries from a plastic container, coke from a can.*

Because her back is to the open entryway, SHE *does not see* JOEL *approach.* HE *raps lightly to signify his presence.*

JOEL: Mom?

SIMONE: *(Startled)* Oh! Why didn't you buzz?

JOEL: I did, a hundred times. The buzzer doesn't work.

SIMONE: *(Kissing him)* Far be it from me, but the buzzer does work.

JOEL *goes to the buzzer on the wall and presses it. From the sound, it appears to work.*

JOEL: *(His chatter indicating deep nervousness about something)* It's the other end that's broken.

HE *laughs.*

I pressed all those other buttons for half an hour. Finally, I hear this voice, this little old lady–

SIMONE: *(Laughing in spite of herself)* Joel! You didn't!

JOEL: She fell in love with me, I guess. Here I am.

HE *takes a folder from his raincoat.*

Is this what you wanted?

SIMONE: *(Taking the folder and wiping it off with a napkin)* Yes. Thanks. I'm sorry I had to bother you.

A beat

The bus was jammed, I suppose.

JOEL: I took a cab.

Quickly

I know, I know – the bus is door-to-door. I don't do buses.

Sniffing out her hamburger.

That smells good.

SIMONE: Take it. I don't really want it.

JOEL: Half.

Breaking the hamburger in two, HE *chooses the bigger half and most of the French fries.*

Why are you showing this place when it's not even your client?

SIMONE: Estelle Byerly's back is out again. I've got all her appointments.

JOEL: This late?

SIMONE: That's when people look for apartments, after they work.

JOEL: *(Going to the window)* It's still coming down in sheets. How come you can't tell in here?

SIMONE: Ground floor rear. You don't see much.

JOEL: This is the "sunny steal?" You need a seeing eye dog.

HE *puts his hands out the window.*

Sheets! My fingers are getting wrinkled!

HE *laughs. Then a beat.*

Mom?

SIMONE: Yes?

JOEL: Nothing.

JOEL *has changed his mind about telling her just yet.* HE *sets off to tour the apartment.*

SIMONE, *looking through the folder, calls out to him.*

SIMONE: Why don't you buy the place, Joel? There's no sale here.

JOEL: *(Offstage)* How do you know?

SIMONE: According to Estelle: "a browser with infuriating questions."

A beat

No kidding, Joel. You could do worse than this little apartment.

JOEL: *(Offstage)* Better than living with you again, right?

SIMONE: I never said that.

JOEL: *(Offstage)* Implied, Mom, implied.

SIMONE: No, really. It wouldn't be a bad investment. Use some of the money your father left you.

JOEL: *(Offstage)* I spent it all on cabs.

SIMONE: I'm being serious.

JOEL: *(Offstage)* Would you waive your commission?

SIMONE: I never waive my commission.

JOEL: *(Returning to the room)* Just testing.

SIMONE: I would co-sign a mortgage.

JOEL: Just what I want. A 30-year loan on a place where you put your hands out the window to find out what to wear.

SIMONE: It would help me to know you think about these things, sometimes. To be on your own. Responsible. Settled.

JOEL: Married.

SIMONE: I never said that.

JOEL: Implied, Mom, implied. You're not eating this, right?

HE *picks up the rest of the meal.*

SIMONE: Still – you can't be willing to do this the rest of your life.

JOEL: This? What this is this?

SIMONE: Moving out, moving in, this job, that job, a hamburger on the run?

JOEL: Mom, repeat after me: "My son is an adult. His return to the nest is temporary. I cannot manage him as though he were a 'fab, sunny steal.'"

SIMONE: Is that what I'm doing?

JOEL: Anyway, it's just till I find something interesting to do with my life.

Getting his courage up now.

Which is closer than you think. I would like you to come with me someplace, Mom.

SIMONE: Now? Tonight?

JOEL: You said there's no sale here. She may not even show.

SIMONE: How do you know it's a she?

JOEL: Maddelena duMornay? That's a she. "A ditzy girl from showbiz," that's what it says in the folder.

SIMONE: You didn't read this file?

JOEL: The cab was stopped for 10 minutes. I had to do something.

SIMONE: The files are private, Joel.

JOEL: Miss duMornay comes to us from Jersey City, which explains things a little bit, doesn't it?

Laughing to hide nervousness.

I've never met a girl from Jersey City. Do they need a passport?

SIMONE: All right, Joel. What is going on?

JOEL: Beats me. What?

SIMONE: When you're nervous about something, you make funny jokes that aren't funny. You become a smart-ass.

JOEL: Is that a fact? I never knew that about myself.

SIMONE: Whatever it is, tell me.

JOEL: *(Dodging the issue)* That girl is some kook! Ask me how I know.

SIMONE: I will not.

JOEL: She's with the North Jersey Symphony Orchestra. Right off, this is none too promising, yes?

HE *waits for a response, but there is none.*

Ask what instrument she plays.

Again, there is no response.

Oom-pa-pa! She plays the tuba! In North Jersey!

SIMONE: So?

JOEL: These are not exactly siren calls, are they?

SIMONE: *(Studying him)* Whatever it is, tell me.

JOEL: *(*HE *has been nailed. After a beat,* HE *places a theatre ticket before her)* This is for you.

SIMONE: What is?

JOEL: An aisle seat.

SIMONE: An aisle seat for what?

JOEL: A play my friend wrote. A girl I like a lot is doing the second lead.

SIMONE: *(Looking at the ticket)* It's staged in a store?

JOEL: A theatre behind a store.

SIMONE: This is the title? "Medea on Madison Avenue?" Talk about ditzy!

JOEL: I thought "ditzy" was Estelle's word.

SIMONE: *(Trying to return the ticket to him)* I don't think so, Joel.

JOEL: The play is really good. We think it would make a film.

A beat

Did you hear me, Mom?

There is no response. HE *gets his next words out quickly.*

I need to borrow some money, Mom.

Very quickly

I've been thinking about it for a while. I need to go back to school.

SIMONE: *(Studying his face)* On the level?

JOEL: Yes.

SIMONE: Then you've had the smartest idea I've heard all year.

JOEL: I know, I know I'm 31, and it's late to–

SIMONE: No, it's not late. If you're serious, it's not. You could try law. Or accounting. You can get an MBA, Joel, and learn real estate. I'll write a check tonight!

JOEL: Only the thing is–

SIMONE: Only the thing is what?

There is no response.

What school are you planning on, Joel?

JOEL: I have more of Dad's money left than you think. I don't need to borrow all that much. $4,000 maybe. I'll live in a dormitory room, I don't mind.

SIMONE: What school?

JOEL: *(Very subdued)* The New York Film Academy.

SIMONE: Oh, God!

JOEL: I think film is my true calling, Mom. I do.

SIMONE: First it was mime! Then it was art history – what was that? This is the same thing all over again.

JOEL: *(Laughing)* What can I do, Mom? I've been touched by a Muse.

SIMONE: Oh, God! It's those Medeas behind the store talking you into things!

JOEL: No.

SIMONE: Now you'll be the oldest living student at the film school.

JOEL: Academy, Mom, Academy. You just said I'm young enough to do anything.

SIMONE: I exaggerated!

JOEL: Come tonight. See the play.

SIMONE: *(Defeated, sad)* No.

JOEL: I'll leave the ticket, okay? If she doesn't show, you'll come, okay? Only, don't be late, okay; they won't seat you late.

Unseen by either of them, MADDELENA DUMORNAY *comes to the open door.*

SHE *carries an unwieldy shopping bag. Everything about her is unwieldy.* SHE *is dressed funny: floppy hat, bulky rain-proofed jacket, fat rain pants, galoshes. A scarf around her head obscures her features.* SHE *looks like a girl from Jersey City who plays the tuba.*

SHE *waits for an opening in the conversation.*

We all have one great hour on earth coming to us. I want mine.

SIMONE: Oh, God! The "one great hour" speech again!

JOEL: *(Looking at his watch)* I have to go. The cab is waiting outside.

Quickly

Only kidding, Mom. I'm being stupid again. I've been worried all day about telling you, that's why.

HE *kisses* SIMONE'S *head.*

MADDELENA: Excuse me. Is Mrs. Byerly here?

SIMONE: *(Standing)* I'm here in Mrs. Byerly's place. She's a little under the weather.

MADDELENA: I'm sorry to hear it.

SIMONE: You're Miss duMornay? Simone Bronfman.

MADDELENA: *(Shaking her hand)* I'm very late, I know. My job kept me longer than I expected. Then, this awful rain! And now, in the lobby? I rang and rang. The buzzer seems to be broken – again.

SIMONE: Is it, really?

JOEL: You're supposed to press all the buttons.

MADDELENA: *(Puzzled by him)* I had to wait for a tenant to show up and let me in.

JOEL: Never! Not in a "fab steal!"

SIMONE: This is my son. He's leaving.

MADDELENA: *(Extending her hand)* Hello.

JOEL: *(Surprised by her firm handshake)* The oom-pa-pa – it's out in the hall, yes?

MADDELENA: I'm sorry?

SIMONE: Pay no attention, Miss duMornay. I don't.

SHE *shoots a stony look at* JOEL.

MADDELENA: I see.

But of course, she doesn't. A beat.

Excuse me.

SHE *reaches into her shopping bag for a newspaper, from which she proceeds to tear page after page.*

Behind her back, JOEL *signals his mother: this one is ditzy!*

But HE *has not been able to "jolly"* SIMONE *at all.* HE *exits, a bit sadly.*

Unaware of all this, MADDELENA *tears her newspapers as a puzzled* SIMONE *watches. Now,* MADDELENA *spreads the pages on the floor as "boats" for her heavily-galoshed steps into the room.*

SIMONE: There's no need for that.

MADDELENA: If this were my apartment and I were trying to find a suitable buyer, I wouldn't want strangers ruining my nice hardwood floors. They could use refinishing though, couldn't they!

Not waiting for an answer, SHE *starts off on her "boats."*

I'll take off these wet things, if I may. The bathroom is this way, as I recall?

SIMONE: Yes, but–

MADDELENA: *(Offstage)* I expected Mrs. Byerly, of course. I hope you won't mind a few questions in her absence?

SIMONE: More questions? It hardly seems possible!

MADDELENA: *(Offstage)* Some co-ops, I've learned, don't own the land they're built on, but lease it on a long-term basis. Which is it here? Can you hear me?

SIMONE: *(Unable to believe her ears)* I can hear you. However, Miss duMornay–

MADDELENA: *(Offstage)* Are we on our own land?

SIMONE: –in my entire professional life, no one has ever asked–

MADDELENA: *(Offstage)* But why not? It's sound consumerism. According to the *Manhattan Land Book* – are you familiar with the *Manhattan Land Book*?

SIMONE: Of course, but–

MADDELENA: *(Offstage)* The *Book* says that if a co-op is on leased land it is generally worth 12-15% less. That's only an average, of course, but one could, perhaps, think of it as a negotiating point, don't you agree?

SIMONE: How do you mean – negotiating point?

Now MADDELENA *appears in the doorway, looking, if possible, worse than before.*

SHE *is wearing a loose housedress over other clothing obviously and unattractively bunched up under it, pinned up, diaper fashion, as we shall see later.* SHE *has a net over her hair.* SHE *is barefoot.* SHE *carries her rain gear over her arm, and then rests it on a chair.*

MADDELENA: Please find out for me, won't you? Also, would you look into why Mrs. Byerly was never able to get a copy of the co-op's initial Offering Plan to me.

SIMONE: *(Still reacting to* MADDELENA'S *appearance)* What? Oh, but this building was co-oped some 20 years ago. It's not that easy to put one's hands on a—

MADDELENA: *(With some difficulty, she takes a thick Offering Plan from the shopping bag, several places bookmarked)* I've been doing my homework.

SIMONE: So I see.

MADDELENA: There is a file of them at the State Attorney General's Office in Albany. I would like to sit down.

SIMONE: Yes, do.

MADDELENA: *(Sitting)* Most potential buyers probably don't ask to see them, but that's not sound consumerism, is it? Besides, why travel to Albany? At 11 W. 42nd Street, between 5th and 6th—

SIMONE: Excuse me, Miss duMornay. But aren't you a – musician?

MADDELENA: Yes, I am. – Avenues, is the Real Estate Institute, which has a Library and Information Center with on-line—

SIMONE: Excuse me, Miss duMornay. A classical musician?

MADDELENA: Yes, I am. Mrs. Byerly said once that in the Manhattan real estate market, apartments are snatched from under your nose in less time than it takes to bother about an Offering Plan. But according to the Real Estate Institute, that isn't true. For a place like this, I mean.

From the shopping bag, SHE *pulls out a colorful bar chart.*

I colored it myself. To clarify.

SIMONE: Has anyone ever told you, Miss duMornay, that it is possible to over prepare?

MADDELENA: Thank you. At any rate, this is a one-bedroom on the West Side. There seems to be a glut of them, Simone. May I call you Simone? And you'll call me Maddelena. Look, here: the average time on the market is 3.3 months.

SIMONE: This is a one-bedroom with dressing alcove.

MADDELENA: A one-bedroom with dressing alcove on the ground floor, however. In the rear. Directly above the noisy furnace area. In a non-doorman building, Simone. Not strong selling features, you'll agree. And, as we both know—

Now SHE *consults a pad.*

–this particular unit has been on the market for 4.3 months.

SIMONE: You must appreciate the special circumstances.

MADDELENA: The owners in Florida and all, yes.

SIMONE: And traveling so much. It's not easy to relay business messages back and forth.

MADDELENA: But that's my point, exactly. They must be anxious.

SIMONE: They are not at all anxious.

MADDELENA: *(From the shopping bag,* SHE *extracts a newspaper article)* Last week, the *Times* Real Estate Section said one of the big problems with elderly people in Florida is their anxiety about leaving unsold property behind. I have no wish to take advantage, but–

SIMONE: They are not anxious. And we've had many offers on the place, Miss duMornay–

MADDELENA: Maddelena. I doubt that that's true.

SIMONE: Serious offers, I might add.

MADDELENA: They can't be very serious, or–

SIMONE: My own son is interested.

MADDELENA: Is he? He didn't strike me as someone who would be. The offers can't have been very serious, or the buzzer would be working, wouldn't it?

SIMONE: I beg your pardon?

MADDELENA: If there had been many buyers making serious offers, you'd never have put up with the delays and the inconvenience, would you?

SIMONE: *(Miffed,* SHE *writes in her pad)* The super will have it fixed by morning.

MADDELENA: Really? He's an unusual super, then. That's a very small bathroom, isn't it. There was barely enough room for my galoshes.

SIMONE: As a matter of fact, it is a large bathroom.

MADDELENA: People have different notions of space, I guess.

SIMONE: *(After a long, scornful look)* Look, Miss duMornay, Maddelena, I have good intuition in these matters, and right now, this all seems like a huge waste of time to me.

MADDELENA: Oh, but it isn't. I am moments away from making my offer. I had no hidden agenda, please believe me, when I said the bathroom is small. It's not a trick to lower the price, or anything – you'd see through such a transparency, isn't that so? But size is a negotiating point, isn't it?

SIMONE: Let's straighten out this business of negotiating points right now, shall we? There aren't any.

MADDELENA: *(Quickly)* If this were my apartment, I'd certainly move the washing machine. Into that hallway, perhaps. It does work?

SIMONE: The wash – ? Of course, it works!

MADDELENA: But since the buzzer doesn't, one can't be sure. I brought a few things of my own to wash, as a small test. You won't mind, I'm sure.

SIMONE: *(Opening her mouth and closing it again, as nothing comes out)* Don't you think that's just a little bit...nervy?

MADDELENA: Nerve is my biggest strength. Fault, if you wish. I do try to manage things. It works against me sometimes. People think I'm trying to manage them. They don't always want managing.

SIMONE: No, they don't.

MADDELENA: Still: things need managing and people, too, sometimes.

SHE *picks up her rain jacket and goes to hang it up.*

This isn't much closet space.

SIMONE: You're forgetting about the side hall.

MADDELENA: You're right. There is a huge closet in the side hall.

SIMONE: Two huge closets.

MADDELENA: One is less huge than the other, isn't it?

SIMONE: They're exactly the same size.

MADDELENA: *(Hanging up her jacket)* The things one doesn't remember when one sees an apartment hurriedly!

SIMONE: You've seen this apartment un-hurriedly. More than once.

MADDELENA: You sound a bit angry with me, Simone. You're not, I hope. The owners might have left the closet organizers, don't you think?

SIMONE: I refuse to talk about closet organizers.

MADDELENA: But, see these screw holes? At regular intervals? There were closet organizers here.

SIMONE: I also refuse to talk about screw holes!

MADDELENA: I just wonder why they'd do it, that's all. A sale is much more friendly when a few sweeteners are left behind. Let me tell you the bind a prospective owner faces right now.

SIMONE: Maddelena, I am trying hard, very hard, and very courteously to–

MADDELENA: Oh, I know. But a prospective owner will have to (a) plug up these screw holes, or (b) buy new closet organizers. Now, new closet organizers may not have screws that line up precisely with these holes. That's a negotiating point, don't you think?

SIMONE: Perhaps you're further away from making an offer than you think.

MADDELENA: This nice table: it goes with the apartment, I understand.

SIMONE: It's up for sale. Everything is up for sale. You knew that.

MADDELENA: I'd forgotten.

Sitting

These nice chairs: do they go with the apartment?

SIMONE: Maddelena! Didn't you just hear me?

MADDELENA: Still: a few sweeteners would be nice, don't you think? May we, Simone, go into the dressing alcove, please? I'd like to clear up a discrepancy in the measurements.

SIMONE: There are no discrepancies.

MADDELENA: But I was given figures: 6 feet, 6 inches by 8 feet.

SIMONE: And?

MADDELENA: The Offering Plan seems to provide different figures: 6 feet, 5 ¾ inches by 7 feet, 11 ¾ inches. A full ¼ inch less on each wall!

SHE *reaches into her shopping bag, and pulls out a measuring tape.*

Perhaps we could measure together?

SIMONE: For ¼ inch?

MADDELENA: Yes.

SIMONE: I think not.

MADDELENA: But why?

SIMONE: *(Again, opening her mouth and closing it again, until)* Aren't you a musician?

MADDELENA: I told you. Yes.

SIMONE: A classical musician?

MADDELENA: Yes.

SIMONE: Then why aren't you – why are you – frankly, I thought you'd be more…more…that is, less…less…

MADDELENA: Less practical? But the dressing alcove, Simone, won't be for dressing. I intend to have my bed there, with a small chest of drawers. They'll fit, but if that extra ¼ inch isn't there, I'll have to have the radiator moved, an added expense. You see?

SIMONE: Just for curiosity's sake, you understand: why on earth would you put your bed into a dressing alcove, rather than the more logical bedroom?

MADDELENA: To cover my expenses. I'll have to rent out the bedroom, Simone.

SIMONE: *(Consulting the folder)* But I understood there was a plan. You were to buy this place with a fiancé.

MADDELENA: *(Matter-of-factly)* That's no longer applicable.

SIMONE: What's no longer applicable? The plan or the fiancé?

MADDELENA: Both.

SIMONE: Both. What happened to the fiancé? He found a way out?

Quickly and genuinely.

I'm sorry. That was rude. I had no right to say that.

MADDELENA: I don't mind. My fiancé was an excellent musician, and I did love him. But he wasn't interested in my calculations, I discovered. Some artists are like that, Simone, they think that the basic business of living is beneath them, and that the world should support their creative work. It should not.

SIMONE: *(Thoughtfully, relating this to JOEL)* No, it shouldn't. I mean, I've heard it shouldn't.

MADDELENA: It makes them – I guess I'd call it – "drift."

SIMONE: Yes. I'd call it that, too.

MADDELENA: I'd have made a good wife, a down-to-earth, common-sense wife. I'd have given him the space for artistry, too. That's another strength of mine, giving people their space. He didn't want my strengths, however.

A beat

So you see? I must rent out the bedroom.

SIMONE: *(Now, SIMONE seems to be turning, has started to go to MADDELENA'S side. A bit contrite now, and much softer toward her)* Maddelena, I know this co-op board. They won't take easily to such an arrangement.

MADDELENA: Oh, but I've pored over the proprietary lease.

From the shopping bag, SHE pulls out a blank lease.

One-bedrooms here allow two residents, maximum. But it doesn't specify related status of residents, you see?

SIMONE: If you're serious…if you're really serious, then, I'll find out. I promise nothing. Nothing, you hear?

MADDELENA: *(Quickly)* Would you also find out, Simone, if the walls between these apartments are truly 12 inches thick, as the Offering Plan says?

SIMONE: WHAT?

MADDELENA: If the walls are 12 inches thick, there can't possibly be complaints about rehearsals.

SIMONE: What rehearsals?

MADDELENA: In my flat in Jersey City, the walls are too thin. Neighbors do hear and do complain, sometimes, and rightly so.

SIMONE *writes it down in her pad.*

(Quickly) Don't forget to ask about the washing machine, too.

SIMONE: *(Getting angry again, standing)* Look here, Maddelena!

MADDELENA: I know, I know. But I need all this information, Simone. I'll have to charge my renter, won't I, for using the washing machine. I can't do that if it isn't working, can I? And as for rehearsals, some friends and I have started a group, a quintet. We'll pick up side jobs, you see? Extra money. It's the blessing of a Manhattan apartment, you know, a central location in which to practice. They'll chip in, just as they've chipped in for rehearsal space elsewhere. Only the cash comes to me. Every little bit helps, yes? Of course, if the walls are not 12 inches thick, drapes can help, wall hangings and things. But they are expensive. That could be a negotiating point, couldn't it?

SIMONE: *(This is a real turning point for her.* SHE *is very impressed. A long beat as* SHE *stares at* MADDELENA*)* You've thought out every bit of this, haven't you?

MADDELENA: I try to make one dollar do the work of two. Is that a strength or a weakness?

SIMONE: A strength. Definitely a strength.

SHE *sits again.*

I suddenly have an odd feeling in my stomach.

MADDELENA: Oh, dear!

SIMONE: I keep thinking about – other people.

MADDELENA: What other people?

SIMONE: Just other people. How impractical they can be – those other people. Not all other people, just – some other people. You know?

MADDELENA: All at once, you seem miles away.

Peering into the food container in front of SIMONE.

Well, no wonder you feel strange. Do you realize the number of fat grams you've consumed?

SIMONE: What?

MADDELENA: The content of the meat, plus the frying oil?

SIMONE: Other people ate most of it. That is – my son did.

MADDELENA: He needs scolding.

SIMONE: You may be right.

A beat

I've never met anyone quite like you before.

MADDELENA: Good or bad?

SIMONE: I'm not sure yet.

MADDELENA: I'm an acquired taste. Like anchovies. After one gets used to them, everybody likes anchovies! Shall we come to grips with this apartment? I am moments away from making an offer!

SIMONE: You are a musician?

MADDELENA: Again?

SIMONE: A classical musician?

MADDELENA: Again? Yes.

SIMONE: It is the tuba, isn't it?

MADDELENA: Well – yes and no, on that one.

SIMONE: Yes and no?

MADDELENA: It's been rather a long day. You won't mind if I have my supper?

From the shopping bag, SHE *takes out two apples and places them on the table.*

Join me, won't you?

SIMONE *shakes her head, no.*

From the shopping bag, MADDELENA *pulls a large knife, and with a deft chop, cuts one of them in two.* SHE *eats as she continues.*

That file of yours is a bit out-of-date. I play several instruments. It was the tuba first and foremost till a few months ago. Then I started keeping a record of my cab fares. Do you know what I learned?

SIMONE *shakes her head, no.*

On a per annum basis, I was spending over $800. Over $800 on cabs alone. If one is to stay in this field, the question becomes: do I want to be in for over $800 per annum on cab fares the rest of my working life?

It would add up to thousands, wouldn't it, unrecoverable thousands of dollars. And so unnecessarily, when one plays other instruments.

SIMONE: It's sound consumerism, I imagine.

MADDELENA: It is! I decided on one of my more practical instruments. And, do you know, I haven't taken a cab in over three months?

SIMONE: *(Perhaps even weakly)* Tonight – in all…this rain?

MADDELENA: I took a bus. It was practically door-to-door! Which is one of the advantages of the West Side over the East Side, ease of transportation. Location, location, location. I think that's what you say.

SIMONE: *(A bit punchy by now)* That's what we say, yes.

MADDELENA: But I shouldn't tell you that, should I? You could use it as a negotiating point against me.

SIMONE: I wouldn't dream of it.

MADDELENA: You want to know if choosing a new instrument has been a financially sound move? Well, it has. I know how fussy co-op boards can be with things like that.

SIMONE: What I want to know, Maddelena, is–

MADDELENA: You want to know if, in spite of my talk about stretching dollars, I can also make the down payment. I can. Years ago, my Aunt Rose, my lovely Aunt Rose, gave me money for my college tuition. "Aunt Rose," I said, "I won't need it. I've decided to win a scholarship to Juilliard." Which I did. "But some day, Aunt Rose, some day, when I need it, your money will be there for me." Well – it's time, don't you think?

An unbelieving SIMONE *does not respond.*

Simone? Is something wrong?

SIMONE: Who are you? Who sent you here?

MADDELENA: What?

SIMONE: Are you some kind of witch?

Quickly

I'm sorry. I didn't mean that. I meant…you're so – I don't know. I expected you to be – I don't know. Other worldly, so to speak. Not quite there, so to speak. From outer space, so to speak.

MADDELENA: Ditzy, so to speak?

Laughing

That's Mrs. Byerly's word. I saw her writing it. I'm not ditzy, though. Am I?

SIMONE: No.

MADDELENA: What I am is – improbable.

SIMONE: Yes, improbable is the word.

MADDELENA: *(Laughing)* But, you see, Simone, these days, in New York, if one is an artist by instinct, one must be a business person by necessity. Improbable – you agree?

SIMONE: I think I do, actually.

MADDELENA: I am moments away from making my offer. Perhaps we can negotiate now.

SIMONE: I know these owners, Maddelena. They won't budge from their price, I'm afraid.

MADDELENA: *(From the shopping bag,* SHE *takes a small pad)* I saw this done on TV once. I am going to put a number on this piece of paper.

   SHE *starts to write.*

SIMONE: No, Maddelena. I don't want you to be disappointed.

MADDELENA: Here is what I can afford.

   SHE *hands the page to* SIMONE.

SIMONE: *(*SHE *reads the number)* I am sorry. It isn't possible.

MADDELENA: Well, of course, it isn't possible. It never is on the first try. If you cross out my number and put down a higher one, slightly higher, we may be closer than you think.

   SIMONE *looks at her for a long time. Conflicted by this girl, her earnestness as well as her naiveté,* SIMONE *at last crosses out the number and puts another one down.* SHE *hands the page to* MADDELENA.

MADDELENA: *(Reading)* I'm sorry, Simone. It isn't possible. My turn again. We keep doing this until it becomes possible. You see?

   SHE *proceeds to write.*

SIMONE: *(Getting angry at herself for going to* MADDELENA'S *side)* No. No. I know what you're after!

MADDELENA: My next figure will be a most attractive one.

SIMONE: No! No! You want me to cut my commission! I NEVER CUT MY COMMISSION!

MADDELENA: I wouldn't ask such a thing.

SIMONE: Yes, you would!

MADDELENA: No. I couldn't.

SIMONE: Why couldn't you? You've asked for everything you could think of. Why couldn't you ask that?

MADDELENA: It wouldn't be right. You've been honest and forthright with me, and you seem to have a begrudging respect for–

SIMONE: I won't listen! I won't! Maddelena, it's not just a question of money. With all your planning and your research…I mean, well, there's nothing for me but to say it. As a friend, really a friend. Frankly…well, frankly, you would never pass an interview with this co-op board.

MADDELENA: Why wouldn't I?

SIMONE: I know what the board looks for. My company has sold over a dozen apartments in this building.

MADDELENA: I can pass any interview.

SIMONE: How? You don't have the slightest idea of how to – that is, a person's appearance counts a little bit, perhaps more than a little bit–

MADDELENA: I can pass any interview.

SIMONE: Not with a ratty scarf around your head. A wrinkled housedress. Bare feet, for God's sake!

MADDELENA: *(Paying no attention to these words,* SHE *writes a new number)* Here's another number for you.

SIMONE: *(Refusing to take the paper)* Not when you dress like a – like a – I'm sorry, I have to say it: like a clown. A clown with a tuba, no less.

MADDELENA: It isn't a tuba anymore. I told you that. And as for my clothes – I just came back from my job. I told you that, too.

SIMONE: Your job. What kind of symphony orchestra allows you to–

MADDELENA: *(Writing one last number)* This is truly and absolutely the highest I can go.

SIMONE: *(Accepting the paper,* SHE *reads and is genuinely saddened)* Then, under any circumstances, it really is not possible, Maddelena.

MADDELENA: *(A long beat.* SHE *is disappointed but brave)* That's it, then, isn't it.

Matter-of-factly.

Well. Well. It seemed to work on TV.

A beat

Well. Well. It is a nice apartment and it would have done me very well–

SIMONE: It's not a nice apartment. It's dark. You have to put your hands out the window to–

MADDELENA: I'd have painted everything white.

SIMONE: But the floors are bad. The bathroom is small. There's no room for your galoshes!

MADDELENA: It's a large bathroom.

SIMONE: There are all these screw holes! Think of that bind a prospective owner faces–

MADDELENA: I know how to fill in screw holes, Simone.

A beat

Well. Well. It won't do to have the soul of a musician but the mind of an accountant, I fear.

SIMONE: No! Don't fear it! Live by it!

MADDELENA: *(Starting to gather up her things)* As for dressing like a clown, Simone, this outfit was meant to be a negotiating point.

SIMONE: *(Sadly)* Maddelena, looking like an old steel wool pad is not a negotiating point.

MADDELENA: If you were to see me as I looked at my work today, you'd have thought, "She moves in elite circles."

SIMONE *would protest.*

Yes, you would have. If you were to see me as I looked today, you'd have thought, "She's stylish. She's rich."

SIMONE *would protest.*

Yes, you would have. I am stylish. I have good taste, I can't help that. But I'm not rich. I couldn't take the chance of looking rich.

SIMONE *would protest.*

MADDELENA *goes to the window and puts her hands out.*

The rain is over. The negotiations are over. It doesn't matter now. I was at PBS today, Simone. We have been taping a holiday special. I hope you'll watch. You'll see that I was dressed very well, indeed.

A beat. SHE *stares at* SIMONE *for a moment.*

This is what your W. 57th Street apartment building will be missing.

SIMONE *will now watch in silent awe as a remarkable transformation occurs before her eyes.*

MADDELENA *reaches into the shopping bag for a lipstick, which she uses.* SHE *removes the ratty scarf, revealing lovely red hair.* SHE *pulls out a pair of red high-heeled shoes, which she puts on. Now* SHE *removes the housedress, uncovering a jeweled red blouse.* SHE *releases the red velvet skirt, which cascades to the floor.* SHE *looks beautiful.*

Well. Well. I do like the apartment. But one must not moon over what one cannot have. It's the only way to survive, isn't it?

MADDELENA *"re-diapers" herself.* SHE *puts the housedress back on.* SHE *retrieves her other stuff and puts it into the shopping bag.*

All the while, SIMONE *is thinking very hard.*

You have been good to me, Simone. I do appreciate it.

Heading for the door.

I hope you agree, at least, that a girl like me deserves not to be from Jersey City.

SIMONE *now "wakes up," as it were, just about the time that* MADDELENA *is at the door.*

SIMONE: Wait!

MADDELENA: Yes?

SIMONE: I want to know something. How old are you?

MADDELENA: You aren't permitted to ask a question like that in a professional capacity.

SIMONE: I'm not asking it in a professional capacity. I'm asking it in a personal capacity. How old are you?

MADDELENA: Twenty-seven.

SIMONE: Twenty-seven. Isn't that something!

MADDELENA *is back at the door.*

Wait!

MADDELENA: Yes?

SIMONE: I want to know something else. Can you look the way you just looked any time you want, or only once in a while?

MADDELENA: I don't think you're permitted to ask a question like that, either.

SIMONE: Tell me, anyway.

MADDELENA: If you mean, do I know how to impress a co-op board–

SIMONE: Yes, a co-op board. But others, too. Men.

MADDELENA: I know how to be attractive, yes.

SIMONE: Isn't that something!

MADDELENA *is at the door again.*

Wait!

MADDELENA: Why?

SIMONE: Maddelena? I want to know one last thing. Your instrument – what exactly is your instrument these days?

MADDELENA: Why would you want to know?

SIMONE: Tell me!

MADDELENA *reaches into her shopping bag and pulls out a flute.*

That? That?

MADDELENA: It's my flute.

SIMONE: Isn't that something!

MADDELENA: Why not? It's cheerful. It's light.

SIMONE: And such an improvement over the tuba! I mean – so feminine!

MADDELENA: That's another reason I gave up the tuba, I suppose. I looked clumsy with it. Women tuba players are the subject of jokes, did you know that?

SIMONE: No, I didn't.

MADDELENA: It's true. Some men – not all men – will actually make jokes behind our backs.

SIMONE: *(Almost to herself)* It's a plot. *(To* MADDELENA*)* Tell me if it's not a plot, Maddelena.

MADDELENA: What on earth are you saying?

SIMONE: I'm saying – I don't know what I'm saying. Tell me this, truly – if you owned this place, you would rent out a room?

MADDELENA: I would have to. But I don't own this place.

SIMONE: And if the person you rented to was well-meaning, and nice, but just a bit – ditzy. What then?

MADDELENA: I don't understand.

SIMONE: If that person were artistic, perhaps, yet badly in need of some reality in his life, you'd find ways to give such a person some of the strengths he needs, your strengths, wouldn't you?

MADDELENA: Would he want my strengths?

SIMONE: He might not, at first. But you could show him the wisdom of your strengths. Gently, quietly. You'd catch him unawares!

MADDELENA: You'd have him – touched by a Muse?

SIMONE: Oh, my God, no! That's already happened! I want him touched by a steel trap! By – an accountant!

MADDELENA: *(A beat)* It's your son, isn't it?

SIMONE: I know a win/win situation when it hits me on the head!

MADDELENA: I don't think it's such a good idea, Simone–

SIMONE: Do you want this apartment?

MADDELENA: Yes, but–

SIMONE: Do you want a recommendation to the co-op board that will get you here in two weeks?

MADDELENA: Yes, but–

SIMONE: Where is that magic pad of yours? Here it is. Now – do you think you could afford the apartment at this price?

SHE *writes a number on the paper, and gives it to* MADDELENA.

There – just like on TV.

MADDELENA: *(Reading)* Oh! Oh!

SIMONE: I have cut my commission in half.

MADDELENA: Oh! Oh!

SIMONE: Well, almost in half. Now – you are going to the theatre tonight. Here's the ticket.

SHE *gives* MADDELENA *the ticket.*

Joel will be sitting on the aisle. After the show, you'll take him to dinner. Here's cash to cover it.

SHE *gives* MADDELENA *money.*

MADDELENA: I couldn't.

SIMONE: I won't have you lousing up your lovely financial reports. Take it!

MADDELENA: *(Taking the money)* Will he enjoy a vegetarian restaurant?

SIMONE: Well, Maddelena, I don't recommend you give him all your strengths at once. Save a few of them for later.

MADDELENA: A turkey burger, then?

SIMONE: Just this once, couldn't it be a big, juicy steak?

MADDELENA: But–

SIMONE: Maddelena, we're talking win/win here!

MADDELENA: I suppose it could be a steak, couldn't it?

SIMONE: Good! Now, listen carefully. I am writing a check. I am not signing it. You'll give it to Joel at dinner. You'll tell him I will sign it on one condition.

SHE *writes a check, and hands it to an unwilling* MADDELENA.

Only this one condition: that, instead of the dormitory room he spoke of, he rents the bedroom you have here. That's all. That's it. Once you give him the check, you're free to enjoy the rest of the evening together.

MADDELENA: But what would we talk about?

SIMONE: Tell him how you manage your budget. Tell him you would manage a budget for a film production just as carefully.

MADDELENA *would protest.*

You can do it, Maddelena! Some things need managing – you said it yourself. People, too! Now – go to the theatre before I realize what a dumb thing I've done. Go on. GO!

MADDELENA *races for her shopping bag.*

STOP! Under no circumstances will you take that bottomless shopping bag with you!

MADDELENA *puts the shopping bag down.* SHE *goes to the closet for her rain jacket.*

STOP! Under no circumstances will you be seen in that industrial strength garment!

MADDELENA *stops in her tracks.*

Now, take off that housedress. Undiaper yourself, or whatever it is you do to get that skirt down where it belongs.

MADDELENA *releases the skirt.*

Put this over your head.

SHE *gives* MADDELENA *a delicate silk scarf from her own neck.*

Don't tie it like that. Drape it over your hair, softly. Let it float.

MADDELENA *follows her instructions.*

Good. Very good. Now–

SHE *gets her own raincoat – white, shiny, stylish – from the closet.*
Put this on.

MADDELENA: I couldn't, Simone.

SIMONE: Trust me on this. Now – get a cab, so you won't be late.

MADDELENA *would protest.*

SIMONE: Just this once. It's not a negotiating point.

At last, MADDELENA *goes out the door. Just when* SIMONE *is about to relax from the strain,* MADDELENA *reappears.*

MADDELENA: We didn't measure. I don't know if my chest of drawers will fit in the dressing alcove.

SIMONE: I'll measure. It'll fit.

MADDELENA: What if the radiator has to be moved?

SIMONE: I'll pay for it.

MADDELENA *goes out the door. As before,* SHE *quickly reappears.*

MADDELENA: The table? The chairs?

SIMONE: They go with the apartment.

MADDELENA: I don't know if the washing machine works.

SIMONE: I'll do a wash for you.

MADDELENA: There's detergent in the shopping bag.

SIMONE: OUT!

> MADDELENA *goes out the door. As before,* SHE *quickly re-appears.*

MADDELENA: My flute! I could never leave my flute behind!

SIMONE: Well, but–

Rethinking

You're right. Show him you're not a tuba player from Jersey City. The flute goes to dinner, too.

MADDELENA: *(Taking the flute, but then stopping at the door)* Simone? What if he doesn't like me?

SIMONE: I know for a fact that he's crazy about anchovies, Maddelena.

MADDELENA: Yes, but–

SIMONE: IF YOU GET OUT OF HERE BY THE COUNT OF THREE, I WILL GIVE UP MY ENTIRE COMMISSION! ONE...TWO...

At this, MADDELENA *scoots out as fast as she can.*

SIMONE *stands there for a second, reviewing what she has done.* SHE *smiles. Then* SHE *dials her cellular phone.*

Estelle? Listen, you are not going to believe this, but it's sold!...Yes! To her. Honest!...Well, she's...no, she's not ditzy. She's improbable, that's all. She's an acquired taste, like – never mind...What? Well, sure I came down...A little. A lot...No, your commission is safe...Mine...I know I never cut mine, but this time, well – we all have one great hour coming to us.... Never mind. I'll call you tomorrow. I have to hang up now...Because I have a wash to do, that's why!

The call is over. Seeing the apple on the table, SHE *smiles and stuffs it into her mouth.* SHE *takes the detergent from the shopping bag, along with a few items for the washing machine. Then,* SHE *stops dead in her tracks.*

Taking the apple from her mouth and looking skyward.

One great hour? Yes?

SHE *puts the apple back into her mouth and heads off to do the wash.*

THE CURTAIN FALLS
END OF PLAY

IN A RIKER'S ISLAND WAITING ROOM

a dramatic monologue

In A Riker's Island Waiting Room

setting:

The waiting area outside the room where the Parole Board will meet to hear the case again.

A small bench is where DANIEL sits or stands as an adult. A rickety table and chair are where DANIEL sits or stands as a child.

time:

The present.

character:

DANIEL, in his early 30s.

The actor will, as an adult, mime being shackled hands and feet. As a child, he is, of course, unfettered.

AT RISE: As the lights come up, DANIEL *sits on a bench, looking at the floor.* HE *holds hands and feet together, as though shackled.*

After a beat, HE *turns to face the audience.*

DANIEL

They always bring me down here by train. From Upstate. Sometimes, while I'm waiting, it's only my hands they cuff. Sometimes, it's my hands and my feet. It depends how they feel at the moment, you know? Today, as you see, I'm considered dangerous! Who knows? Maybe I am.

A beat

Sometimes, while I'm waiting, there's a guard breathing down my neck. Sometimes, he stands by that door, in front of the hearing room. So I won't get any ideas, you know?

HE *laughs*

Why the hell would I? Where the hell would I go?

A beat

This is my... my eighth review before the panel of experts. Or my ninth? You lose track. It doesn't matter: they won't let me go. I don't blame them.

A beat

You want to hear about bureaucracies? I'm still in the files as "juvenile." I mean it! In a file seven inches thick, and on every page, stamped, in bright red ink: "Juvenile Offender." How can you still be a juvenile offender when you're a hundred years old? Don't ask me. Ask them.

A beat

The experts on the panel may change over the years, but not what they want from me. They won't let me go. I'll tell you why. Two things they want from me; I can give them only one. They want to see "mental-rehabilitation-slash-personality-integration", which is all one thing and which I can give them, and do give them. It's the other thing I can't give them: remorse. No, I can never give them that. I wasn't sorry then, when I did it, and I'm not sorry now, today. It doesn't matter. They won't let me go. I don't blame them. What do you think of that?

A beat

I think today is Momma's birthday. I'm not sure, because I still get that day all mixed up in my head. Did I bring home the gun on her birthday, or on the day before? I don't remember. Was I eleven or twelve? I don't remember that, either.

HE *stands and shuffles, as though shackled, to a table in the middle of the room.* HE *sits. Now eleven or twelve years old again,* HE *is unshackled, able to move hands and feet freely.*

See this table? I found it on the street one day. Somebody actually threw it out, you know? I carried it upstairs, to be our desk. I mean, on TV, boys had desks in their bedroom, so why shouldn't Billy and me have one, too? And in the drawer...?

To his unseen younger brother.

Billy, you should be asleep, you know you should!... I'll show it to you, but only if you promise not to tell, okay? ...Because it's a surprise for Momma... And you can't touch it, okay? ...Because you're too little. Only I can touch it.

From the drawer, HE *takes a revolver and puts it on the table.*

...It depends, Billy. If he doesn't wake up when Momma comes home from work, I don't have to. But if he does wake up, and he starts in, then I have to... Yes, I do think it's a good thing, Billy, because we don't want her to go through that any more. Not the hitting, not the kicking, and not the–

This is painful to say.

–the belt with the buckle, because that's the worst... And, it's a good thing, too, because then, see, he won't ever lock the door on us again. I can't stand that any more... No, the gun is only a loan, Billy, a loan – don't you know what a loan is? ...From my friend...It's his father's gun, and he doesn't even know we took it, and you must never tell.

HE *withdraws a bullet from the drawer.*

...What? ...No, the bullet can't be a loan, Billy, because you use it and then it's gone... No, I didn't have enough money to buy more... My lunch money...A few weeks – how do I know how many lunches I missed?... Sure, it's worth it! To know Momma won't have that belt with the buckle on her face anymore!

HE *loads the gun.*

You can watch me load it, yes, but only if you stay way over there, okay?... You press here with your finger and you point it. Then, there's the explosion and whoever you point it at, he falls over, like on TV... Sure, we'll be happy! Billy, listen now, go to sleep, you hear?... You can't watch it, no, because there might be stuff and you shouldn't see it, okay? ...Okay, but just one song, because she'll be home any minute, and then, if he wakes up, and he starts in, and he locks the door on us...

As HE *sings, he points the gun in various directions.*

Singing

> "Sleepy boy, sleepy boy, won't you
> Go to dream now?
> When you wake, the sun will bake,
> So won't you go to–"

Billy? Are you asleep, Billy?

His brother asleep, DANIEL *returns to his bench, shackled, morose.* HE *turns to the audience again, the grown man once more.*

The lock on the door? If he turned it, we would know he was going to start in on Momma. She would come home from her night job at the hospital, and she would open our door a little, to see we were all right. I'd try to stay awake if I could, so I'd feel her warm kiss on my forehead. Then, she might put a little present on the desk for us – yellow candies, or little red cars, or something. Momma would buy them for us, only – only, I would hear Daddy yelling at her sometimes that she didn't buy them, that this man working at the hospital, who...who–

A beat. This, too, is painful for him to recall.

–liked her, and bought things for her and for us, too. And then – Daddy would lock our door. And, he would start in. And then – I don't know why, my hands would start–

A beat

–shaking, just shaking, something he did not like, and whenever he saw it, he'd get even madder.

His hands start to shake. HE *looks directly at the audience.*

My God, my hands! It was twenty years ago – why would my hands–?

A beat. HE *crosses back again to the table. A child again,* HE *speaks to his mother.*

Hi, Momma! ...No, I wanted to wait up so I could tell you: I have a birthday present for you... It's a surprise... Later... What's that? A milk truck? A red car? That will be for Billy. I'll put it under his pillow... He likes us, doesn't he, Momma, that man? He likes us more than Daddy does... Yes, I will try not to wet my underwear again. I will... Momma? Be very quiet, please, okay, so you don't wake him up?

A beat. DANIEL *goes to the bench again.* HE *is an adult again, at the bench, looking into the audience.*

It would begin with a whispering in the bedroom. Then, it would get louder, not Momma – she had a soft voice. But him, Daddy: his would get louder and louder, and Momma would cry. And then... and then... there would be noises, like slaps and kicks. I would hear little noises from

Momma's throat. Then... then, if it was really bad, it would be that belt, the belt with the big buckle, and she would scream, she would scream!

A beat

And then I would try to wake Billy up, because I didn't want to listen to it alone. I couldn't listen alone, you know?

HE *goes back to the table, reverting to childhood again.*

Billy? Billy? Wake up! Here's a red car! Don't you want to see it?... Billy! Don't sleep! Please! Billy! He's coming to lock the door!

Although at the table, HE *is an adult again, facing the audience once more.*

Sometimes, I could run out before he locked it, and try to stop him. I'd try to grab his arms, but he was so strong, so strong... I could never... I could never... He'd throw me back into the room and lock the door. That's when it would get really bad. I'd hear this click, this little click, and then–

A click is heard. DANIEL, *hearing it, becomes a screaming child again.*

Oh, no, Daddy, no. Awwh, don't! She didn't do anything. Look: My hands are shaking again. Punch me, Daddy. Me! I'm the one making you mad! Please! Please! Awhh, Daddy, don't. Don't!!!

A long beat. DANIEL *is an adult again.*

Afterwards, he would come back, and unlock the door, and I think that click was worse, because in the kitchen Momma would be hurt, really hurt and bleeding, and he would never let me help her, get her a glass of water or anything. So, the second click was worse.

We hear that second click now, indicating that the door has at last been unlocked. DANIEL *picks up the gun.* HE *is calm, passive, unfeeling about what he is going to do, the child again.*

You stay in here, Billy. I'm going to give Momma her birthday present now. No, stay in here. Here I come, Momma. You're going to be happy now, Momma, I promise.

HE *walks to the front of the stage.* HE *points the gun and shoots, the sound reverberating.* HE *lowers the gun.*

HE *walks back to the table and puts the gun on it.* HE *shuffles back to his bench.* HE *sits down, reverting to his shackled status.* HE *turns to the audience.*

It's two things they want from me, and I can only give them one. Remorse? I can't give them remorse, because if I were eleven or twelve again right now, and Momma needed me, I would do it all over again.

An unseen guard makes a sound that engages his attention.

Me? You want me?

To the audience.

They're ready for me inside.

HE *starts back, then turns to the audience again.*

I would do it again, I know I would.

To the unseen guard.

Yes, I'm coming!

To the audience.

They won't let me go. I don't blame them. It doesn't matter.

HE *shuffles to the back of the stage.*

THE CURTAIN FALLS
END OF PLAY

.

CONSTANZA LO CICERO
AT THE BOATHOUSE IN CENTRAL PARK

a one-act play

Constanza Lo Cicero
At The Boathouse In Central Park

production history:

In November 1998, this play was presented by Gettis/Jacobson Productions at The Piano Store, New York City. It was directed by Jody Jacobson with the following cast:

Constanza . . . . Lisa Risano
Raimondo . . . . .Frank Delconte

In May 2000, this play was presented by Theatre With Your Coffee in Miami, Florida. It was directed by Jen Ryan with the following cast:

Constanza . . . . Lisa Boggio
Raimondo . . . . Michael MacEachem

Constanza Lo Cicero at the Boathouse in Central Park was presented in a staged reading by Stageplays Theatre Company, on January 21, 2002, at Repertorio Español, in New York City. *Constanza Lo Cicero at the Boathouse in Central Park* was presented as part of an evening of two one-act plays exploring issues of multiculturalism in our society. The play, presented in association with The Hispanic Organization of Latin Actors, was directed by Tom Ferriter, with Rob Rodriguez as the narrator and the following cast:

Constanza . . . . Victoria Malvagno
Raimondo . . . . .Gilberto Arribas

setting:
A bench in Central Park.

time:
A late afternoon in June.

characters:
CONSTANZA, 28
RAIMONDO, 27

AT RISE: The bench is empty. A pretty but heavy-set girl comes on. Wearing an ill-fitting bridesmaid dress, SHE *carries the wedding bouquet she has just caught.*

SHE *sits, looking straight ahead for a moment, seemingly composed.* SHE *is not composed; she suddenly begins to wail. Now, a young man enters. Tall, thin, the guest-who-went-overboard-on-his-tuxedo,* HE *watches the girl. Then, hesitantly,* HE *sits on the far end of the bench.*

RAIMONDO: *(At long last)* Are you all right?

HE *gets no response.*

Can I help?

CONSTANZA: Go away. That will help.

RAIMONDO: *(Standing, starting off sadly, but giving it one more chance)* Is there another thing I can do?

CONSTANZA: You've done enough already.

RAIMONDO: I? What have I done? What?

CONSTANZA: *(Getting a bit teary again)* As if you didn't know.

RAIMONDO: I don't know. I don't.

CONSTANZA: Ask those friends of yours at Table 12.

RAIMONDO: You mean my co-workers?

CONSTANZA: Who cares what they are! Oh, don't think I didn't see them laughing. The whole table, laughing at me!

RAIMONDO: No! Never!

CONSTANZA: They dared you, right? "Follow her to the ladies' room! Get her to dance!"

RAIMONDO: Never!

CONSTANZA: "Place your bets! $5 the fat one dances with him, $10 she doesn't."

RAIMONDO: There were no bets, I swear it!

CONSTANZA: "$20 if she dances and one of her boobs falls out!"

RAIMONDO: There was nothing like that. On my honor!

CONSTANZA: You didn't call out, "Dance with me!"?

RAIMONDO: Yes, I did.

CONSTANZA: You didn't call me a name?

RAIMONDO: Never!

CONSTANZA: A bad name!

RAIMONDO: I called you–

CONSTANZA: Never mind. I don't want to know! Well, what can you expect at a yuppie, power-player wedding, for God's sake!

RAIMONDO: It's not just an ordinary, everyday wedding?

CONSTANZA: *(Not really listening)* Not only a yuppie wedding, but a yuppie wedding at a yuppie boathouse in a yuppie park, which, for God's sake, I didn't even know they allowed weddings at a boathouse!

RAIMONDO: I didn't know it, either.

CONSTANZA: Well? There are 100 thin, know-nothing yuppie girls in there, just dying to dance with the tall Hindu in the tight tuxedo.

RAIMONDO: I'm not a Hindu.

CONSTANZA: Muslim, then.

RAIMONDO: I'm not a Muslim.

CONSTANZA: Then why are you swarthy?

RAIMONDO: Swarthy?

CONSTANZA: Don't you know you're swarthy? Don't you know what swarthy means?

RAIMONDO: Yes, I know what swarthy–

CONSTANZA: Don't speak to me. Not one word. You could be a rapist. A Lithuanian rapist. How do I know?

RAIMONDO: I'm not. Either one.

CONSTANZA: Who cares? Who cares what you are? I don't know you, I don't want to know you, and I don't know what you want from me.

RAIMONDO: I want to dance with you. That's all, Connie.

CONSTANZA: How do you know my name?

RAIMONDO: The bride called you "Connie." When she threw the bouquet.

CONSTANZA: *(Looking at the bouquet)* Who wants it? Who needs it?

RAIMONDO: *(A beat)* Don't you want to know my name?

CONSTANZA: No.

RAIMONDO: It's Raymond.

CONSTANZA: Raymond! A white bread name! A WASP name! A WASP name for a WASP pretender!

RAIMONDO: I'm Latino.

CONSTANZA: Raymond? Latino? Hah!

RAIMONDO: I anglicized. For you.

CONSTANZA: Don't anglicize for me. I've had it up to here with anglicizing, Mr. – Ramon.

RAIMONDO: Raimondo. Raimondo Ramirez.

CONSTANZA: *(A beat)* So how is this supposed to work?

RAIMONDO: How is what supposed to work?

CONSTANZA: I don't care what you've heard in there, my name is Constanza.

RAIMONDO: It's a nice name. I like it.

CONSTANZA: Constanza Lo Cicero. How about that?

RAIMONDO: How about what?

CONSTANZA: Lo Cicero: Italian. Ramirez: Latino, if you're to be believed. Italians don't salsa. Latinos don't tarantella. So there you are. How is this supposed to work?

RAIMONDO: *(Mulling this over)* Is it always this complicated at yuppie, power-player weddings?

CONSTANZA: Yes! Yes, it is!

SHE *adjusts the low-cut dress as best she can, wailing again.*

This dumb dress!

RAIMONDO: The dress is lovely.

CONSTANZA: *(Blowing her nose)* And don't start asking about signs, either. I do not believe in signs. You do, I suppose.

RAIMONDO: I won't ask you about signs, Connie.

CONSTANZA: Because I'm a Gemini, and Geminis don't believe in signs. That's undisputed fact.

Blowing her nose again.

So? Which side are you?

RAIMONDO: I beg your pardon?

CONSTANZA: I'm speaking English, Mr. Ramon Ramirez.

RAIMONDO: Raimondo Ramirez.

CONSTANZA: Are you from the bride's side or the groom's side?

RAIMONDO: The bride's, yes.

CONSTANZA: I knew it, I knew it!

RAIMONDO: You knew it?

CONSTANZA: Why wouldn't I know? The groom is my brother. I've met all his friends. I deduced.

RAIMONDO: Deduced?

CONSTANZA: Haven't you ever deduced? "Elementary, my dear"–

RAIMONDO: Raimondo.

CONSTANZA: Oh, this is risible. Risible!

RAIMONDO: This "risible," is it a bad thing?

CONSTANZA: Oh, please. This is some Latino stunt. No more, okay? Just because I've relocated, don't think I've forgotten the ways of this tricky city.

RAIMONDO: Relocated?

CONSTANZA: Don't you know what "relocated" means, either, Mr. Ramon Whatever?

RAIMONDO: Raimondo. Raimondo Ramirez. And yes, I do know.

CONSTANZA: You must be a distant relative, a very distant relative, because the bride is most certainly not Latina, is she! You're a fourth cousin? A fifth cousin, perhaps?

RAIMONDO: I'm not related.

CONSTANZA: I knew it! I knew it! Not her. Not her. Before she'd have a Latino cousin, she'd grow a creampuff on her ass!

Embarrassed by her own words.

I don't often use vulgarity, but there is no other way to say it.

RAIMONDO: Don't you like Elizabeth?

CONSTANZA: Elizabeth? Elizabeth Anne? What's to like about an Elizabeth-Anne? Oh, those English, with their mis-chie-vi-ous hearts.

SHE *has, of course, mispronounced.*

RAIMONDO: Mis-chiev-ous.

CONSTANZA: What?

RAIMONDO: You said mis-chie-vi-ous. It's mis-chiev-ous.

CONSTANZA: I did not say mis-chie-vi-ous. I said malicious. Those proper English faces hide malicious hearts, didn't you know that?

RAIMONDO: No. I didn't.

CONSTANZA: Well, they do.

Scornfully

Elizabeth Anne Pearson Lawrence. What kind of name is Elizabeth Anne Pearson Lawrence?

RAIMONDO: I like that name.

CONSTANZA: She talked him into it, you know. Oh, malicious, malicious heart!

RAIMONDO: Talked who? Into what?

CONSTANZA: My brother. Into the name change.

RAIMONDO: Oh.

CONSTANZA: *(Scornfully again)* Lawrence. Anthony Lawrence. What's wrong with Antonio Lo Cicero, I want to know. It's high Italian, the highest Italian, good enough for a Roman, a famous Roman, Cicero. I suppose you haven't heard of him.

RAIMONDO: He was a power-player.

CONSTANZA: Definitely, a power-player.

RAIMONDO: Still: it means "wart," you know.

CONSTANZA: What means "wart?"

RAIMONDO: Cicero.

CONSTANZA: What? Who told you such a crazy story?

RAIMONDO: It's true. This great orator, with a wart on the tip of his nose, which is why they called him Cicero.

CONSTANZA: I've heard of stupid things in my life, but this! This really takes the cake. What are you? Anti-Italian?

RAIMONDO: No, of course not.

CONSTANZA: Then no more false rumors about Italian warts, all right?

RAIMONDO: No more.

CONSTANZA: Antonio: it was good enough for him for 26 years. Now, suddenly, it isn't. How come? I'll tell you how come: it doesn't go with Elizabeth Anne. Out Antonio, in Anthony. Out Lo Cicero, in Lawrence. Elizabeth Anne and Anthony Lawrence, white bread yuppie power-players, married in sin!

RAIMONDO: Married in sin?

CONSTANZA: Is this a church? This is a boathouse! A boathouse, for God's sake!

RAIMONDO: I like a wedding in a boathouse.

CONSTANZA: Oh, you like everything! Stop liking everything, okay?

Beat

Send him to college to learn something. What does he learn? He learns how to find the Elizabeth Annes of the world! What is it with these English women, anyway? She didn't put him through college. I did!

RAIMONDO: She's very nice to me.

CONSTANZA: When is she nice to you?

RAIMONDO: Every day. At the company. Where we work.

CONSTANZA: I knew it! I knew it! Another yuppie power-player!

RAIMONDO: *(Not by any means humbly)* I work in the Mailroom.

CONSTANZA: *(Laughing)* The Mailroom!

RAIMONDO: What's wrong with the Mailroom?

CONSTANZA: And you thought you could ask me to dance? Oh, it's risible!

RAIMONDO: Risible?

CONSTANZA: Laughable!

RAIMONDO: *(Dejectedly)* Oh.

CONSTANZA: For your information, Mr. Ramon Ramirez–

RAIMONDO: Raimondo. Raimondo Ramirez.

CONSTANZA: For your information, Mr. Ramon Ramirez, unlike other Italian girls you might annoy at a boathouse, Constanza Lo Cicero has also been to college, which it is fairly obvious you have not!

RAIMONDO: Do you have to go to college to dance?

CONSTANZA: *(Not listening)* Oh, it may not be considered necessary for girls in Italian families to go to college, but she did.

RAIMONDO: You did? I mean, she did?

CONSTANZA: All the money at home, of course, went to little brother, so he could go to an out-of-town college and be a yuppie power-player. But big sister outwitted them, didn't she! When they thought she was working overtime at night? She was going to community college! One whole year! Learning words like "risible!"

RAIMONDO: Your vocabulary is wonderful. I mean, hers is.

CONSTANZA: Did she stop there? Constanza Lo Cicero did not.

RAIMONDO: She didn't?

CONSTANZA: She went on to do this astonishing thing, this really astonishing thing.

RAIMONDO: She did?

CONSTANZA: She relocated. Oh, yes. To a civilized part of the country.

RAIMONDO: Where did you – where did she relocate?

CONSTANZA: *(Not listening)* Her company asked her to relocate, pleaded with her. Oh, yes. What do you think now?

RAIMONDO: I think that's wonderful.

CONSTANZA: She snapped at the chance to leave this hellhole of a city. Oh, yes. What do you think now?

RAIMONDO: I think that's–

CONSTANZA: *(Caught up in her own story)* "I will go," I said. "I see the need and I will go." I only flew back here yesterday, you know. I can't wait to get on the plane, to get back to polite civilization!

RAIMONDO: Polite civilization?

CONSTANZA: *(Looking at him, proud to tell)* Corinth, Mississippi.

RAIMONDO: I think that's wonderful.

CONSTANZA: It is.

RAIMONDO: You – I mean, she – I mean you became a yuppie power-player, Connie!

CONSTANZA: I did. That's exactly what I did!

Beat

So you see why it's impossible for me to dance with the Aztec from the Mailroom.

RAIMONDO: I'm not an Aztec.

CONSTANZA: A swarthy mail boy, from a table full of mail boys! Swarms of them, making fun of people, laughing as they guzzle their "servicios" one after the other.

RAIMONDO: *"Cervezas." Cervezas*, one after the other.

CONSTANZA: Making insulting remarks about – about–

SHE *looks down at her dress and begins to cry again.*

What is it with her, anyway, to order a dress like this, when I have relocated and can't attend a fitting? Oh, malicious, malicious English heart!

RAIMONDO: But it's such a nice dress.

CONSTANZA: She had it shipped in from Taiwan. She must have. They never get things right.

RAIMONDO: They don't?

CONSTANZA: Was it made for a woman? It was not. It was made for a beanpole. Am I a beanpole?

RAIMONDO: You are, as we say, *guapa*, Connie. That's what I called out to you. "Dance with me, *guapa!*" You see?

CONSTANZA: *(Not listening)* She's the flagpole! Eat everything in sight and never put on an ounce. Oh, malicious Elizabeth Anne Pearson Lawrence!

RAIMONDO: Actually, she eats very little. I bring her lunch sometimes.

CONSTANZA: Well, of course she eats very little! How can she eat a thing, that's what I'd like to know, with her conscience bothering her?

RAIMONDO: Her conscience?

CONSTANZA: Surely you know what she does for that power-player HMO you work at. She refuses people the operations they desperately need.

RAIMONDO: No, Connie.

CONSTANZA: And when her type refuses an operation, it stays refused!

RAIMONDO: But I hear her on the phone. She never refuses operations.

CONSTANZA: Her type refuses operations only when nobody's around to hear her refuse them.

RAIMONDO: *(Dejectedly)* I am very confused right now.

CONSTANZA: Of course! Because you think everybody is wonderful and everything is wonderful!

SHE *looks at the bouquet in her hands and holds it out to him.*

Get this straight, Ramon.

RAIMONDO: Raimondo.

CONSTANZA: I did not try to catch it. She put it into my hands. Malicious, malicious!

SHE *throws it into the nearby garbage can. Up like a shot,* RAIMONDO *tries to retrieve it.*

Don't you dare!

RAIMONDO: It's bad luck!

CONSTANZA: Bad luck? Who says it's bad luck? Where do you get these screwy ideas?

RAIMONDO: *(Dejectedly)* I don't know.

CONSTANZA: Leave it.

A beat

And why are you still here, bothering me?

RAIMONDO: *(Looking at his watch)* There's time, Connie. We could go inside.

CONSTANZA: And what?

RAIMONDO: And dance.

CONSTANZA: Again? Again with the dancing? How many times do I have to tell you it isn't going to work? Listen to that awful music. Such noise! *Troppo rumoroso* is what we say.

RAIMONDO: *Muy ruidoso* is what we say.

CONSTANZA: What?

RAIMONDO: You said what you call noisy music, so I said what we call–

CONSTANZA: Stop! You see how different the words are? You see how impossible it all is?

RAIMONDO: *(Dejected,* HE *turns away from her)* I think you're right. It's not going to work.

HE *gets up and starts to go.*

CONSTANZA: *(Not wanting him to go,* SHE *actually softens a bit)* Actually... you aren't that swarthy, are you?

RAIMONDO: *(Turning around, encouraged)* I'm not?

CONSTANZA: Now that the sun is behind the clouds, I see you more clearly.

RAIMONDO: *(Overjoyed)* Right! Right!

CONSTANZA: Still – it's not going to work.

RAIMONDO: Why not?

CONSTANZA: Because there is always trouble between people like us, who come from ocean areas.

RAIMONDO: I beg your pardon?

CONSTANZA: From ocean areas. Seas. It means trouble, always, which is why Antonio Anthony Lo Cicero Lawrence is going to have trouble being married to Elizabeth Anne Pearson Lawrence. He'd be better off with a Ukrainian.

RAIMONDO: A Ukrainian? But the Ukrainians have a sea. The Black Sea.

CONSTANZA: The Black Sea is nowhere near the Ukraine. Don't you even know that? Besides–

RAIMONDO: Besides what?

CONSTANZA: Cold seas don't count. It's the warm seas that cause all the trouble.

RAIMONDO: *(Thinking this through for a moment)* But – but Miss Pearson is – I mean, the North Sea isn't a warm sea.

CONSTANZA: How do you know? Do you go around taking the temperature of oceans and seas?

RAIMONDO: No.

CONSTANZA: I didn't think so.

RAIMONDO: *(Trying to digest all this)* You know a lot about bodies of water.

CONSTANZA: Well, I should, shouldn't I?

RAIMONDO: You should?

CONSTANZA: I work for the *National Geographic*, don't I?

RAIMONDO: You do?

CONSTANZA: Why do you think I relocated to Corinth, Mississippi? Don't you recognize a career move when you hear one?

RAIMONDO: A career move?

CONSTANZA: We're worlds apart obviously, just worlds apart. It's risible.

RAIMONDO: *(Dejectedly)* Are you a power-player writer at *National Geographic*, Connie?

CONSTANZA: No.

RAIMONDO: A power-player photographer, then?

CONSTANZA: I'm an Administrative Assistant.

RAIMONDO: I see.

CONSTANZA: Administration is just as important to the success of the *National Geographic* as any power-player writer or power-player photographer, make no mistake.

RAIMONDO: No question about it.

CONSTANZA: All right, then.

Beat

My area of expertise is Fulfillment. Subscription Fulfillment. I suppose you don't know what that is.

RAIMONDO: I don't.

CONSTANZA: Well, then. As I said, we're worlds apart.

Beat

I have my own accounts.

RAIMONDO: You do?

CONSTANZA: In addition to having the single largest cubicle on the fourth floor and having six girls reporting to me, and overseeing the entire Label Room...well, I have my own accounts.

RAIMONDO: It sounds important.

CONSTANZA: It is important. *Importante*, you would say.

RAIMONDO: Yes, I would say that.

CONSTANZA: I have a title, too. Subscription Address Change Consultant.

RAIMONDO: I think that's wonderful.

CONSTANZA: I'm in full charge of address changes for Muslims and Hindus, and do you know why? Because they have incredibly difficult names. What do you think of that?

RAIMONDO: I think you're definitely a power-player.

CONSTANZA: I mean, any idiot can do decent names. It takes brains to do Muslims and Hindus.

RAIMONDO: I see that.

A beat, as HE *thinks up names to match her "image."*

I have trouble with Czechoslovakian names myself.

CONSTANZA: What kind of screwy thing is that to introduce into this conversation? You see what I mean?

RAIMONDO: I just meant–

Dejectedly

Nothing.

CONSTANZA: Okay, then. But think about this, please: if you had a subscription to *National Geographic* and you changed your address, would you want your label entrusted to someone who doesn't know what she's doing?

RAIMONDO: Never!

CONSTANZA: Well, there you are!

RAIMONDO: I'm going to get a subscription on Monday, I swear it.

CONSTANZA: Well, good.

RAIMONDO: *(A beat as* HE *thinks. Then, triumphantly)* Connie! We can dance! I'm not from an ocean. Or from a sea! I'm from a gulf! My family comes from the Gulf of Mexico!

CONSTANZA: *(Maybe even with a bit of sadness)* There's trouble with any body of warm water.

RAIMONDO: Oh.

A beat as HE *thinks again. Then, triumphantly again.*

But I have my own accounts, too.

CONSTANZA: I hardly think it possible for a mail boy to have his own accounts, is it?

RAIMONDO: It is! I deliver mail on floors 53 to 58 only, letters G to N only!

CONSTANZA: It's hardly the same thing, is it?

RAIMONDO: But there are more G to Ns than any other letter in the alphabet!

CONSTANZA: Then it is possible, I guess.

Having digested this, SHE *starts to wail again.*

Oh, but it isn't fair, Raimondo.

RAIMONDO: You called me Raimondo.

CONSTANZA: Did I?

RAIMONDO: But what isn't fair?

CONSTANZA: Everything! You arrive from no place, from a gulf, from floors 53 to 58, letters G to N only. You follow me outside, you practically kidnap me, like an Albanian terrorist!

RAIMONDO: I'm not Albanian. I'm not a terrorist!

CONSTANZA: *(Not listening)* A hired gun is what you are!

RAIMONDO: A hired gun?

CONSTANZA: Hired by that malicious English heart! Oh, I know her ways, I see through her dark plan: she's doing a piece of work here, winning me over, matchmaking, inviting you to entice me to your side and to her cause!

RAIMONDO: I think she did not, Connie.

CONSTANZA: You think she did not, but you don't know she did not.

RAIMONDO: She invited all of us, the entire Mailroom. A to F, O to S, T to Z, everyone at Table 12!

CONSTANZA: Don't I know that? Don't I? That's her cover. So we wouldn't suspect the schemes, the conspiracies!

RAIMONDO: There are none, Connie.

CONSTANZA: No? Then why are you tall and thin? Why are you fairly lovable? And almost handsome, which you know. You know you're almost handsome, admit it!

RAIMONDO: *(A beat)* Yes. I know I'm almost handsome.

CONSTANZA: There. You see?

RAIMONDO: But I don't merchandise my good looks, Connie. I don't want to be a power-player with my good looks.

CONSTANZA: *(Not listening)* Oh, it's war, total war. Expect no quarter, give no quarter! Admit something else: admit you want to dance with me to see if one of my boobs falls out of this dress.

RAIMONDO: *(Shamefacedly)* Yes. I admit it.

CONSTANZA: You see? War, total war!

RAIMONDO: But that's only one reason.

CONSTANZA: *(Sadly)* Both of them, then, Raimondo? You want both of them to fall out? Oh, crude, cruel and crude!

RAIMONDO: No! No! I only – that is, when I saw you, I thought, "She's nice, very nice."

CONSTANZA: *(A beat)* You did?

RAIMONDO: I still think so.

CONSTANZA: You do?

RAIMONDO: Yes.

CONSTANZA: Why?

RAIMONDO: Why? There's no why. You looked nice then and you look nice now.

CONSTANZA: Oh.

SHE *has trouble taking this in, believing him.* SHE *stands.*

No. No, no, no, no. When I passed by to the ladies' room? The whole table, that whole mis-chie-vi-ous Table 12 was laughing.

RAIMONDO: Yes.

CONSTANZA: At me.

RAIMONDO: No.

CONSTANZA: Yes, Mr. Ramon Ramirez.

RAIMONDO: Raimondo Ramirez.

CONSTANZA: Mr. Raimondo Ramirez, Mr. Macho, Latino Mailboy, Crude, Possible Albanian Terrorist Ramon Raimondo Ramirez: you were making jokes about me. A table of mail boys laughing at a visitor from Mississippi!

RAIMONDO: They were not, Connie.

CONSTANZA: Oh, it's war, total war.

RAIMONDO: *(Quietly)* They were laughing at me. Because – because I was foolish enough to repeat something my uncle who raised me taught me.

CONSTANZA: *(Not listening)* Both barrels between the eyes!

RAIMONDO: When I went to my first dance? My uncle who raised me said, "Raimondo? We're *hombres* – men – and men have it easier than *mujeres* – women. So while you're having fun at the dance"–

CONSTANZA: Of course! Have your fun with the unsuspecting *mujeres*!

RAIMONDO: "Look around," he said, "for a lady who is not having a good time. Dance with her. You'll feel better."

CONSTANZA: *(A beat.* SHE *is touched but hides it)* Oh, I knew it! I knew it! Charity!

RAIMONDO: No, Connie.

CONSTANZA: Well, Mr. Raimondo Raised By His Uncle Ramirez, Ms. Constanza Lo Cicero of the *National Geographic* Fulfillment Department does not need charity!

RAIMONDO: *(Very dejectedly)* I told it to you all wrong.

CONSTANZA: *(A beat. Then seriously)* Anyway: why did they laugh at that? It's sweet.

RAIMONDO: They laughed because of my codicils and provisos.

CONSTANZA: Codicils and provisos? HMO talk! What provisos?

RAIMONDO: I've never been able to do it, Connie, what my uncle who raised me said: dance with the lady who's not having a good time – unless – unless–

CONSTANZA: Unless what?

RAIMONDO: Unless the lady meets three conditions.

CONSTANZA: What conditions?

RAIMONDO: First, she has to look intelligent.

CONSTANZA: I've been told I look intelligent.

RAIMONDO: You do look intelligent.

CONSTANZA: And the second condition?

RAIMONDO: I like for her to have melting kindness in her eyes. Like a doe's.

CONSTANZA: I've been told I have melting kindness in my eyes, like a doe's.

RAIMONDO: Yes. You do.

CONSTANZA: And the third condition?

RAIMONDO: I will not ask for a dance with one of those power-player model types, all skin and bones, with sharp and pointy angles, no hips, no–

HE *is about to say "boobs."*

I don't want to say the word.

CONSTANZA: What word?

RAIMONDO: Well, the lady must have–

HE *cups his hands at his chest.*

We call them *los pechos.*

CONSTANZA *grows silent. We see a sudden, slow smile creep across her face as* SHE *realizes her "candidacy."* SHE *sits up, very, very straight. Then, just as suddenly,* SHE *frowns; still, it is with a far less abrasive attitude that* SHE *speaks.*

CONSTANZA: One duty dance, right? Lift the poor *mujeres* up and knock them down again, right?

RAIMONDO: I would never do that, Connie.

CONSTANZA: *(A long beat)* What's your sign?

RAIMONDO: I don't know.

CONSTANZA: Well, what's your birthday?

RAIMONDO: October 28.

CONSTANZA: I knew it! I knew it! Scorpio! Scorpios are liars, always were liars, always will be! Oh, it's risible. It won't work. It can't work!

RAIMONDO: I'll change my birthday, Connie. May. February. Whatever you want.

CONSTANZA: Is that what you Latinos do?

RAIMONDO: All the time. All the time!

CONSTANZA: *(A beat while* SHE *thinks this through)* No. No, no, no.

RAIMONDO: Why not?

CONSTANZA: An Italian can spot it right off: there's something wrong. There is a lie lurking somewhere!

RAIMONDO: But there isn't.

CONSTANZA: You're married.

RAIMONDO: I'm not married.

CONSTANZA: To a Communist.

RAIMONDO: I don't know one.

CONSTANZA: A Chinese Communist!

RAIMONDO: All the Chinese Communists are in China!

CONSTANZA: You have illegitimate children. There are *muchachos, muchachos*!

RAIMONDO: I have no children.

CONSTANZA: You're gay, then. You're one of those – *maricons*!

RAIMONDO: I'm not gay. I just want to dance, Connie.

CONSTANZA: You just want to dance. Oh, it's war, total war! Till the last bullet is fired!

RAIMONDO: Why do you keep saying that?

CONSTANZA: Because, it's too perfect. Nothing can be this perfect! There's something, Mr. Ramon Raimondo Ramirez. There's always something–

RAIMONDO: Nothing. I swear it.

CONSTANZA: ALL RIGHT, THEN! ALL RIGHT!

More calmly.

One dance. Just one.

CONSTANZA *takes* RAIMONDO'S *arm.* THEY *begin to walk across the stage. Suddenly* CONSTANZA *stops.*

No Mexican hat dances! I hate them.

RAIMONDO: None. I promise.

CONSTANZA: No Polish polkas! I hate them.

RAIMONDO: None. I promise.

CONSTANZA *takes his arm again.* THEY *resume the walk across the stage. Suddenly* CONSTANZA *stops again.*

CONSTANZA: Afterwards, you'll leave me in the corner. Breathless, gasping, without resources! Done, finished, *finita*, from the noisy music!

RAIMONDO: But just listen, Connie. They're not playing noisy music any more.

CONSTANZA: *(As* SHE *listens)* They're getting tired, that's all.

RAIMONDO: It's soft music. Sweet music.

CONSTANZA: *Dolce*, we say.

RAIMONDO: *Dulce*, we say.

CONSTANZA: *(Sweetly)* But that's – practically the same word, Raimondo!

RAIMONDO: You see?

CONSTANZA: Then, maybe, it could work, couldn't it!

CONSTANZA *takes* RAIMONDO'S *arm.* THEY *begin to walk across the stage. Then suddenly* RAIMONDO *stops.*

RAIMONDO: Connie? Is withholding a truth the same as lying?

CONSTANZA: Yes, it is. It most definitely is!

RAIMONDO *starts to walk with her again. Then* HE *suddenly stops.*

RAIMONDO: Then, Connie? There is something.

CONSTANZA: I knew it! I knew it! What did I just say? What did I just tell you?

RAIMONDO: I'm not exactly what you see.

CONSTANZA: Of course not! They never are. Oh, it's war, total war! No prisoners will be taken!

RAIMONDO: A few years back, Connie? I had this sort of change. It was important for me. You see?

CONSTANZA: I knew it! I knew it! You're a woman, right? You wear that tight tuxedo, like some macho Latino, but–

RAIMONDO: That's not it.

CONSTANZA: Then what? WHAT?

Slowly, wordlessly, stretching out this moment of truth, RAIMONDO *reaches into his breast pocket.* HE *pulls out a yarmulke and puts it on his head.*

CONSTANZA: Oh, God! Oh, God!

RAIMONDO: You don't approve, right?

CONSTANZA: It's the *hora* you want me to dance!

RAIMONDO: I don't know how to dance the *hora*, Connie.

CONSTANZA: Oh, God! Oh, God!

RAIMONDO: Is it – is it risible to you, Connie?

CONSTANZA *is speechless.* SHE *stands there, staring at the yarmulke.*

(HE *is crushed*) It won't work. I see that now.

RAIMONDO *starts off alone. There is a long beat as* CONSTANZA *watches his progress. Of course, by now,* SHE *does not want him lost to her.*

CONSTANZA: Wait! Raimondo? This – conversion of yours? Did it take place near the ocean? The sea?

RAIMONDO: *(Smiling)* It was definitely an inland conversion.

CONSTANZA *walks toward him.* THEY *start off together. Suddenly,* SHE *breaks away from him and runs back toward the bench.*

RAIMONDO, *sure now that all is lost, shakes his head sadly and starts off alone.*

CONSTANZA: WAIT! WAIT!

RAIMONDO *stops and turns to look at her.*

CONSTANZA *reaches into the garbage can and retrieves the bouquet.*

My God! Why are you Jews so impatient?

Seeing RAIMONDO'S *uncertainty,* CONSTANZA *smiles –* SHE *has, after all, made a joke, her only joke of the day, the kind of joke that signifies magnificent progress for her.*

RAIMONDO *realizes the joke's significance, too.* HE *smiles.*

CONSTANZA *takes* RAIMONDO'S *arm.* THEY *go off together.*
Stopping and listening.

Oh, just listen to that music, Raimondo! It's so–

RAIMONDO: *Dolce*, you say.

CONSTANZA: *Dulce*, you say.

THEY *exit together.*

THE CURTAIN FALLS
END OF PLAY

TWO OLD MEN TALKING IN A McDONALD'S IN PLAINVIEW

a one–act play

Two Old Men Talking In A McDonald's In Plainview

production history:

TWO OLD MEN TALKING IN A MCDONALD'S IN PLAINVIEW was presented in September 2000 by Stageplays Theatre Company at the South Oxford Space, in Brooklyn, New York. It was directed by Tom Ferriter with the following cast:

Murray . . . . .Jerry McGee
Cortland . . . . .Jack Frankel

This play was presented in a staged reading by Stageplays Theatre Company, on February 6, 2001 at The Episcopal Actors' Guild, in New York City. TWO OLD MEN TALKING IN A MCDONALD'S IN PLAINVIEW was presented in an evening of three one-act plays exploring issues of our urban environment under the umbrella title *East End – West End: Three Tales of Manhattan.* The play was directed by Tom Ferriter, with Danielle Cautela as the narrator and the following cast:

Murray . . . . Barnard Hughes
Cortland . . . . Thomas Barbour

In November 2003, this play won First Prize in the Great Neck Public Access TV competition; since then, it has been shown repeatedly on Long Island and area public access TV channels. It was directed by Norman Hall with the following cast:

Murray . . . . Marvin Einhorn
Cortland . . . . Michael Rosenthal

TWO OLD MEN TALKING IN A MCDONALD'S IN PLAINVIEW was subsequently presented in a staged reading by Stageplays Theatre Company, on December 8, 2003, at The Lambs, in New York City. TWO OLD MEN TALKING IN A MCDONALD'S IN PLAINVIEW was presented in an evening of three one-act plays exploring issues of aging in our society under the umbrella title *October Stories.* The play was directed by Tom Ferriter, with Allison Abrams as the narrator and the following cast:

Murray . . . . Thomas Barbour
Cortland . . . . .Jerry McGee

setting:
A typical McDonald's interior in a typically urban locale.

time:
The present, morning.

characters:
MURRAY, 70
CORTLAND, 60

AT RISE: MURRAY *sits at a table doing the crossword puzzle in his newspaper. His dress is somewhat slovenly.* HE *sips coffee from the container before him.*

CORTLAND *passes, carrying his breakfast tray.* HE *is well-dressed in jacket and tie. Recognizing* MURRAY, HE *stops at the table.*

CORTLAND: Murray. Am I right?

MURRAY: *(Tentatively)* Right.

CORTLAND: Then, hello. It's good to see you!

MURRAY *barely nods.*

You do remember me?

MURRAY: Should I remember you?

CORTLAND: Cortland Price? Cort? Mercy Hospital? My Elaine, your – I forget your wife's name.

MURRAY: Ada.

CORTLAND: Ada! Elaine and Ada, Room 705.

A beat

17 months ago. What happens to time?

MURRAY: It passes.

CORTLAND: I'll join you, yes, Murray?

A not overly enthusiastic MURRAY *moves his newspaper.*

17 months. What have you been doing with yourself, Murray?

MURRAY: Not so much.

CORTLAND: Your line of work: I forget what it is.

MURRAY: Dry cleaning.

CORTLAND: Dry cleaning, yes! Two stores. I do recall that.

MURRAY: Three.

CORTLAND: Three. And? Are they doing well?

MURRAY: I don't know.

CORTLAND: You don't know?

MURRAY: I sold them to my partner. I pulled out.

CORTLAND: You pulled out? Why?

MURRAY: Why not?

CORTLAND: Was it wise of you? To give them up at this time?

MURRAY: I don't know. Was it wise?

CORTLAND: To have a place to report to regularly – that's important, Murray.

MURRAY: A place to report to? In the morning I report to McDonald's for breakfast. In the afternoon I report to McDonald's for lunch. If I don't finish the puzzle at breakfast, I finish it at lunch. Isn't that wise enough for you?

CORTLAND: But not filling your days each day? Not taking part in what life has to offer us?

MURRAY: "What life has to offer us." You're – what? 10 years younger than me? You tell me: what has life to offer us?

CORTLAND: The going on, surely.

MURRAY: *(Blankly)* The going on, surely.

CORTLAND: Bravely, one hopes.

MURRAY: *(Blankly)* Bravely, one hopes.

CORTLAND: My Elaine insisted, always: "I want you to go on, Cort." Your Ada wanted you to go on, too.

MURRAY: I thought that's what I was doing.

CORTLAND: I mean, Murray, to be productive, to do things, real things. To keep occupied.

MURRAY: My coffee keeps me occupied. My puzzle keeps me occupied.

CORTLAND: Something with structure, Murray. "A woman's day fills itself. A man's day is filled for him." That's what my Elaine used to say.

MURRAY: Is that what your Elaine used to say? My Ada didn't used to say that.

A beat

CORTLAND: Your children? Daughters, weren't they?

MURRAY: Sons.

CORTLAND: You do see them?

MURRAY: One lives in Chicago, the other in Kansas someplace.

CORTLAND: I see my daughter every day. I took an apartment around the corner from her. I have a little grandson.

HE *reaches into his wallet for a picture.*

MURRAY: I can do without that.

CORTLAND: His name is–

MURRAY: *(Matter-of-factly,* HE *puts his hand over the picture)* I said I can do without that.

CORTLAND: *(A patient beat)* You're still depressed, then. Am I right?

MURRAY: Which I shouldn't be. Am I right?

CORTLAND: Up to a point, Murray.

MURRAY: And what point is that?

CORTLAND: We had a terrible time, a terrible, terrible time. Elaine, Ada. Chance roommates. Angry illnesses. But Murray, 17 months ago. 17 months!

MURRAY: I can count, Cort.

CORTLAND: "Dear, dear Cort," my Elaine said, "don't grieve too long. I won't have you grieving too long."

MURRAY: Your Elaine seems to have talked a lot; my Ada didn't.

CORTLAND: As soon as I could, then, I went back to my work. You recall my work?

MURRAY *shakes his head.*

Philosophy and the Humanities. At the University. I'm surprised you don't remember.

MURRAY: Some days, I don't remember to put my socks on.

HE *raises one foot, sneakered but not socked.*

Huh! Today is one of them.

CORTLAND: *(Laughing, then consulting his watch)* Look at the time! I'd best get at this muffin, don't you think?

MURRAY: *(Watching a moment, then a bit sarcastically)* So how come you're not eating a perfect breakfast at your productive home? Didn't your Elaine leave instructions about that?

CORTLAND: *(Patiently)* It's okay, Murray.

MURRAY: Or how come you're not eating a perfect breakfast at the University? At the fun-filled Philosophy and Humanities table?

CORTLAND: *(Determined not to be upset)* It's okay, Murray. I understand. I do. I don't see my classes Wednesday morning. On Wednesday mornings, I attend "Group."

MURRAY: "Group?"

CORTLAND: The hospital told you about "Group," didn't they? They gave you the literature.

MURRAY: When it was time to get out of there, I got out. I didn't wait for literature.

CORTLAND: "Group" was formed for people like us, Murray, people in the aftermath, so to speak.

MURRAY: So to speak.

CORTLAND: I joined "Group" the day after my Elaine died. You hear the word, "died?" Most people will say "passed away" or "moved on" or "left me." In "Group," I learned to say the word "death," face the word "death." It was a real breakthrough.

MURRAY: A breakthrough, right!

CORTLAND: I joined "Group" because I knew myself, Murray. I wanted to go forward.

MURRAY: I see that.

CORTLAND: It's very important to know yourself.

MURRAY: I see that, too.

CORTLAND: Such a wreck when I began, Murray. So lost! Today? I'm president of the "Group."

MURRAY: Isn't that something!

CORTLAND: Elected president, three months ago!

MURRAY: Congratulations on the victory.

CORTLAND: By unanimous vote.

MURRAY: Congratulations on the unanimous vote.

CORTLAND: One of my responsibilities is to look for ways to help people. That's what a president does.

MURRAY: Is that what a president does?

CORTLAND: I've got a brochure right here.

HE *pulls one from his pocket.*

My idea. Would you believe before I was president they didn't have a New Members brochure?

MURRAY *puts his hand over the brochure, shaking his head.*

It could be helpful to you, Murray.

MURRAY: I'm not much for reading.

CORTLAND: Promise me you'll look at it later.

MURRAY: No. I don't promise.

CORTLAND: There's a sentence here just written for you. "In the larger sense, our marriages serve to equip us to live alone, for we know that one partner will survive the other."

MURRAY: I can do without that.

CORTLAND: "Our job as loving spouses, then, is to acknowledge that, to act on it."

MURRAY: I said I can do without that!

CORTLAND: *(Patiently)* I'm trying to help you, Murray. Just yesterday, in the library, I happened on some interesting research. I discovered what certain ancient cultures did to restore perspective when a loved one died. Let me tell you.

MURRAY: Will they mind if I drink my coffee while my perspective gets restored?

CORTLAND: Directly after the ceremonies, the family came together to make a list: all the faults of the loved one. Not the virtues, you understand, the faults.

MURRAY: The faults. Got it.

CORTLAND: The faults, Murray, are the key.

MURRAY: That's the key. Got it.

CORTLAND: Why only the faults?

MURRAY: It beats the hell out of me.

CORTLAND: Because when a loved one dies, we tend to mythologize.

MURRAY: Mythologize. Of course!

CORTLAND: We remember our Elaines, our Adas, as flawless people, with every positive feature, every lovely trait. But our Elaines, our Adas were not flawless, Murray. That is not real life.

MURRAY: Not real life, no.

CORTLAND: The listing of faults is designed to block the tendency to mythologize. Block the tendency and healing will begin. You see?

MURRAY: Healing will begin. I see that, yes.

CORTLAND: Direction can return, you see?

MURRAY: Direction can return. I see that, yes.

CORTLAND: I'm going to present the idea to "Group" today. Of course, it's supposed to be done immediately after the ceremonies, so any list you and I might make now won't have the same impact.

MURRAY: Good. We won't bother then.

CORTLAND: *(Pulling out a paper)* Would you like to hear the list I've made of my Elaine's faults?

MURRAY: No. I would not.

CORTLAND: But why not?

MURRAY: For openers, your Elaine might not like it.

CORTLAND: She'd be the first to encourage it.

Reading

#1: Elaine had a temper. She'd become angry with me, for no reason I could see. Not many people knew that. It was my cross to bear.

MURRAY: She was ill, Cort.

CORTLAND: Before she was ill. #2: Elaine would sometimes pretend she was reading a book I had recommended, but she wouldn't read it.

MURRAY: She was ill, Cort.

CORTLAND: Before she was ill. #3: Elaine would go for days without making herself up, unless there was someone else around.

MURRAY: She was ill, Cort.

CORTLAND: Before she was–

MURRAY: I don't want to hear any more. Okay?

CORTLAND: #4: Elaine was not a neat person. Her side of the closet was always the messy one. She never closed a drawer or a cupboard correctly. She never stacked the newspapers for recycling properly.

MURRAY: A woman who is ill should recycle properly?

CORTLAND: Before she was ill. #5–

MURRAY *puts his hand over the paper.*

I have two more.

MURRAY: No.

CORTLAND: But–

MURRAY: No! They are not faults.

CORTLAND: They are faults.

MURRAY: They are what human beings do.

CORTLAND: You're not getting the point. The point is to–

MURRAY: The point is to not mythologize, I get that, I get it! My God, Cort!

CORTLAND: But–

MURRAY: But! But! But WHAT? My Ada made noises when she slept. Some women get prettier when they get older. My Ada stopped being pretty when she was 25. My Ada was cranky, the pain in her legs made her cranky. But Cort, Cortland, Cortland Price! She was a person, a person! It all goes with the territory.

CORTLAND: I understand what you're going through, Murray, but–

MURRAY: But what? I was married to her for 44 years. Every morning of her life, she said the same thing. "Murray! Sit down when you eat!" Every morning! I missed her saying that 17 months ago and I miss it now. I was angry at her for leaving me – pardon me, dying! – then, and

I am angry at her for leaving me – pardon me, dying! – now. But I know she didn't want the pain in her legs any more, so some day I'll stop being angry. Okay? OKAY?

CORTLAND: Come to "Group," Murray.

MURRAY: "Group?" Is "Group" going to fill the big hole in me where Ada was? I want her to say to me, "Murray! Sit down when you eat!" one more time. I want someone to say it. Who? You? Will you say it?

CORTLAND: Murray, I–

MURRAY: Say it! Say "Sit down when you eat!" SAY IT!

CORTLAND: You are sitting down.

MURRAY: Say it, anyway!

HE *stares at* CORTLAND. *Then* HE *covers his face with his hands.*

CORTLAND: Come, Murray?

MURRAY: No. Here is where I come. Here is where I do my crossword puzzle. Tomorrow I'll do another. It's what I have now, what I know about now, okay? I'll do a puzzle every day and maybe one of those days I won't remember what she looked like. Okay? Okay? You, Cort, my friend, Cortland Price, president: do your Humanities and Philosophy classes, make your list of faults, go to "Group" all you want to, say "death" all you want to, "she died, she's dead" all you want to, be occupied, be very occupied. You have ten more years than I have to fool yourself.

MURRAY *and* CORTLAND *sit and stare at each other for a long moment. Then* MURRAY *stands.*

(*Quietly*) It's time for me to go home. There's nothing to do there, but at this time of the day, I go home. It's what I do to begin the next part of my day.

CORTLAND *continues to stare at him.* MURRAY *starts off, then comes back and shakes* CORTLAND'S *hand.*

To have a grandson around the corner is a nice thing.

MURRAY *exits slowly.*

CORTLAND *sits staring after him for a long moment.* HE *looks at the list in his hand for another long moment.*

CORTLAND: (*In a whisper*) Elaine! Elaine! Why did you – why did you – leave me?

THE CURTAIN FALLS
END OF PLAY

ON AN UPTOWN LOTTERY LINE

a one-act play

On An Uptown Lottery Line

setting:
Exterior, stationery store, located in Harlem.

time:
A late afternoon in Fall, as a slight shower is just ending.

characters:
AARON, 15

MAX, 30

MR. PHILLIPS, 45

MONA, 25

BOBBIE, 45

JACK, 30

MALE PASSERBY

FEMALE PASSERBY

YOUNG MALE PASSERBY

AT RISE: Four people wait on line outside the store to buy lottery tickets. Dollar bills, as well as the numbers THEY *will play, are clutched in their hands.*

AARON, *first in line, is nervous, watchful, protective of his place in line.* HE *keeps his distance from* MONA, BOBBIE, *and* JACK, *the "regulars."*

MALE PASSERBY *tries to join the line. This elicits a well-practiced routine from the "regulars."*

MONA: *(Calling out)* So what's holding things up?

BOBBIE: *(Calling out)* Let's shake it, okay? Let's move it, okay?

To the PASSERBY.

Everything's slowed up here.

MALE PASSERBY: What's the trouble?

BOBBIE: Their machines have broken down again.

MONA: *(Puffing on a cigarette)* It's a computer virus.

MALE PASSERBY: Computer virus! That's ridiculous!

BOBBIE: No. The same thing happened last week. There's a place three streets down. If I could walk better, I'd go there.

JACK: *(Calling out loudly)* Get this fucking show on the fucking road, all right?

Happy with his role in all this, HE *smiles at the* PASSERBY, *who impatiently goes off.*

HIS *exit elicits a "high five" from the "regulars."*

MR. PHILLIPS *comes along, with open umbrella, attaché case, and detached air.* AARON, *spotting him, pulls up his collar, and tries not to be seen.*

MONA: *(Calling out as before)* So what's holding things up?

BOBBIE: *(Calling out as before)* Let's shake it, okay? Let's move it, okay?

To MR. PHILLIPS.

Everything's slowed up here.

MR. PHILLIPS: *(Folding his umbrella,* HE *doesn't even look at her)* Let me by, please.

BOBBIE: Their machines have broken down again.

MONA: It's a computer virus.

MR. PHILLIPS: I said, let me by!

BOBBIE: The same thing happened last week. There's a place three streets down. If I could walk better–

MONA: *(Seeing* MR. PHILLIPS *without umbrella for the first time)* Mr. Phillips! It's you!

JACK: *(Calling out loudly, as before)* Get this fucking show on–

MONA: No, Jack.

Gesturing to the others to leave off the routine, she turns to MR. PHIL-LIPS.

Mr. Phillips! Don't you remember me?

MR. PHILLIPS: *(Gesturing toward the check in her hand)* Whoever you are, young lady, you'd do well to keep that welfare check out of sight.

MONA: Oh, it's all right, Mr. Phillips. They cash them here.

A beat

Don't you know me? Mona? My son, with the hearing problem?

MR. PHILLIPS: *(HE doesn't remember)* Oh, yes. How is he?

MONA: Deaf never goes away, Mr. Phillips.

Embarrassed not to remember her, MR. PHILLIPS *moves away a bit to retie a loose shoelace.*

He doesn't remember.

BOBBIE: Who is he?

MONA: My case worker. At the agency.

Beat

It was only a few months ago. He should remember.

BOBBIE: Those guys? They never remember.

MONA: I remember. Speeches! Nothing but speeches, day after day!

BOBBIE: Did you listen?

MONA: Does it look like I listened?

SHE laughs, and shows her big belly. Deciding on a moment of revenge, SHE pushes out her belly at MR. PHILLIPS.

Look, Mr. Phillips. It didn't take.

MR. PHILLIPS: I beg your pardon?

MONA: You sent me to Family Planning. It didn't take.

MR. PHILLIPS: More's the pity, young lady.

MONA: Wish me luck this one will hear, you know?

MR. PHILLIPS: Keep smoking like that and I doubt it.

MONA: *(A beat. Then a resigned smile)* What the hell. You know?

SHE *takes a new cigarette from* BOBBIE'S *pack, and lights it from her own cigarette.*

BOBBIE *laughs, and* MONA *joins in.*

MR. PHILLIPS, *shaking his head, takes money from his pocket and heads for the store.*

AARON: *(Hiding his face in his scarf)* You can't go in right now.

MR. PHILLIPS: I want my newspaper.

AARON: The computer experts are in there.

MR. PHILLIPS, *shrugging, starts to walk away.* HE *stops and studies* AARON.

MR. PHILLIPS: *(HE opens a notepad and flips through it)* Aaron? It is you! Why aren't you at your interview?

AARON: I can't let you in here. The computer experts are fixing the machines.

MR. PHILLIPS: Never mind that. What about your interview?

HE *consults his notes again.*

Home Depot. 4 o'clock. Why aren't you there?

AARON: I was.

MR. PHILLIPS: And?

AARON: There was no job.

MR. PHILLIPS: What do you mean, no job? I spoke to them myself.

HE *consults the notepad.*

You were to talk with the stock manager.

AARON *shrugs.*

Why are you here?

AARON: I'm holding this place for somebody.

MR. PHILLIPS: For whom?

AARON: For my friend. I owe him a favor.

MR. PHILLIPS: What favor?

AARON: He took me to Home Depot. I didn't know how to–

MR. PHILLIPS: I told you how to get there. I wrote it down.

AARON: I lost the paper.

MR. PHILLIPS: *(Feeling under* AARON'S *collar)* The paper is still there. Where I pinned it!

AARON: I needed Max. I do better when Max is—

MR. PHILLIPS: Not much better, since you didn't get the job.

AARON *shrugs.*

There is no Max. There is no favor. You're on this line with these... these others...to buy lottery tickets.

AARON: No.

MR. PHILLIPS: No? What's that in your hand?

AARON: Some numbers.

MR. PHILLIPS: What for?

AARON: A ticket. Just one ticket.

MR. PHILLIPS: One ticket is one too many for a boy who won't stay in school and won't take a job.

AARON: They don't want me either place, Mr. Phillips.

MONA: *(Lowering her voice)* What's taking Max so long?

BOBBIE *shrugs.* SHE *offers* MONA *another cigarette.*

(Taking the cigarette) What the hell.

MR. PHILLIPS: Throwing away your money! All our talks, Aaron. I thought we were making progress. We are not making progress at all.

HE *reaches for the paper in* AARON'S *hand.*

And these are the numbers you'll play, I suppose?

HE *reads from the paper.*

You call this handwriting, Aaron? 116...18...91...Why do these numbers look so familiar?

AARON *shrugs.*

That's my social security number! How did you get it?

AARON: I copied it. I like to copy numbers.

Simply and ingenuously.

I copy words, too.

MR. PHILLIPS: Where did you see these numbers?

AARON: At the Agency. On the wall.

MR. PHILLIPS: What wall?

AARON: The toilet wall.

MR. PHILLIPS: My social security number is not on the toilet wall, Aaron.

AARON: Not your toilet. The toilet we use.

BOBBIE: *(Calling out)* Tell them to clean once in a while!

SHE *laughs her hacking laugh.*

MR. PHILLIPS: *(Taking other slips from* AARON*)* My address! My telephone number!

BOBBIE: *(Calling out)* Those are not good numbers. My boyfriend played them last week.

SHE *turns an unlucky thumb down.* MONA *joins her in raucous laughter.*

MR. PHILLIPS: You're coming with me!

AARON: I can't.

MR. PHILLIPS: You're coming with me and telling me exactly what happened at Home Depot!

AARON: I did.

MR. PHILLIPS: You did not! Shall I call your mother then?

AARON: No!

MR. PHILLIPS: Well?

AARON *gives in.* THEY *move to a new corner.*

JACK: Get this fucking show on the fucking road, all right?

BOBBIE: Jack! When somebody comes by! Only when somebody comes by!

MR. PHILLIPS: Listen to them, Aaron! Do you want to grow up to be one of them? Do you?

AARON: I don't know.

MR. PHILLIPS: You do know! Show me one, just one intelligent person here. You can't. Intelligent people know lotteries are no answer. It's a sucker's game, Aaron – and all the sadder because they don't know it. Am I right?

AARON: I don't know.

MR. PHILLIPS: You do know! Dreaming that a ticket, a number, will take them out of a dreary mountain of debts. Brought on by their own stupidity in the first place. Maybe if they read a book once, instead of making book!

AARON *shrugs.*

BOBBIE: *(To* MONA*)* I see what you mean about the speeches.

MONA: You ain't heard nothin' yet!

MR. PHILLIPS: Responsibility? None. Ambition? None. This store isn't selling lottery tickets, Aaron. It's selling illusions.

MONA: *(To* BOBBIE*)* Funny. I never noticed that. Did you?

BOBBIE: *(Loud enough for* MR. PHILLIPS *to hear)* Can I put illusions on my credit card, Mister?

MONA *and* BOBBIE *share another boisterous laugh.*

MR. PHILLIPS: Stupid, loud, pregnant, again, for God's sake, when they can't afford the children they have!

HE *looks through his attaché case.*

All the same! All of you! Excuses! Excuses and sad stories! Blame everybody but yourselves!

HE *finds* AARON'S *papers.*

Yes, I did. I knew I did. Less than four hours ago, I gave you money. Didn't I do that?

AARON: *(Quietly)* Yes.

MR. PHILLIPS: You needed it to get to the interview. You said that. Didn't you?

AARON: *(Quietly)* Yes.

MR. PHILLIPS: I gave you cash from my own pocket. Didn't I?

AARON: *(Quietly)* Yes.

MR. PHILLIPS: Two weeks ago, I gave you cash from my own pocket to buy your school supplies! That wound up on the lottery line, too, didn't it!

AARON: I guess so.

MR. PHILLIPS: *(Looking at* AARON'S *record)* You guess so. Your own mother accuses you of stealing money from her. Do you know what the agency calls that? Incorrigible. Incorrigible. Read it. Go ahead! Read it!

HE *shoves the paper into* AARON'S *face.*

AARON: I don't want to!

HE *pushes the papers away.*

BOBBIE: Jesus! Does he ever stop?

MONA: Never.

MR. PHILLIPS: You will have her come see me, Aaron. Tomorrow.

AARON: She can't.

MR. PHILLIPS: Why not?

AARON: She's in the hospital.

MR. PHILLIPS: Is she! When did she go into the hospital?

AARON: I don't remember.

MR. PHILLIPS: When?

AARON: I don't remember!

MR. PHILLIPS: *(A beat)* Is that the truth? Is it?

AARON nods.

Softening

You might have told me. We have no secrets from each other, you and I. Will she be all right?

AARON shrugs.

I am sorry about your mother, Aaron. I hope you believe that. She will be all right, I know.

A beat

I get tired sometimes. I mean–

A beat

If your mother's sick, it's all the more reason you need to keep your money. Not throw it away. Forget this favor, this friend. Come. Maybe we can save the job.

Unseen by MR. PHILLIPS, MAX comes out of the store. His appearance on the scene occasions whispering between MONA and BOBBIE, a big smile from JACK.

There is something vaguely dangerous about MAX. HE wears a hefty overcoat with a bulging pocket. HE is obviously hiding a weapon.

AARON, seeing him, pulls out of MR. PHILLIPS' grip and races back to his place in line.

MAX: *(Ominously low-keyed with AARON)* This is how you keep my place? This is how you repay me, friend?

AARON remains silent. MAX indicates MR. PHILLIPS.

Who is he?

AARON whispers into his ear.

To MR. PHILLIPS.

So, you're Mr. Phillips. Hello, friend.

HE holds out his hand to MR. PHILLIPS, but the gesture is rejected.

MR. PHILLIPS: *(To AARON)* Tell your friend I'm not his friend.

AARON: He calls everyone "friend," Mr. Phillips.

MAX: I do that, friend. I do. Aaron's told me a lot about you.

HE holds his hand out again, and is again rejected.

MR. PHILLIPS: Tell him you're coming with me, Aaron.

MAX: Well, now, that's not possible.

MR. PHILLIPS: Why?

MAX: I sort of need him here for a while.

Turning to JACK.

Take Aaron's place, okay, Jack?

JACK *happily does so.*

It's time for you to help inside now, Aaron. First, bring out two cokes, would you do that? One for Mr. Phillips and one for me? I think he wants to have a conversation with me.

MR. PHILLIPS: I think I don't want to have a conversation with you.

MAX: *(Still to* AARON*)* And a toasted cheese sandwich for me.

HE *gives* AARON *coins.*

Leave this on the counter, if Poppy is – you know, tied up or something?

MONA, BOBBIE *and* JACK *roar with laughter at this.*

AARON: *(Whispering, very worried)* Don't tell him!

MAX: What would I tell him?

AARON: About me. Or Momma.

MAX: Why would I tell? You're a friend.

AARON *goes toward the store.* MAX *takes a cell phone out of his coat.*

To MR. PHILLIPS.

This is Poppy's phone. He lent it to me. That's what we call him, "Poppy," which is funny, because he's like no Pop you ever saw. An East Indian, with a turban. And a big family upstairs. And a fondness for cell phones.

Into the phone.

Hello, computer experts? Our young friend is on his way in, you got that? How are things going in there?...Well, good... Put Aaron on it. He'll get it right.

HE *puts the phone away and turns to* MR. PHILLIPS. HE *gestures toward some boxes as possible seats.*

MR. PHILLIPS: No.

HE *moves toward the store.*

MAX: I can't let you in there, Mr. Phillips.

HE *gestures to the seats again.*

Ten minutes. I'll tell you a few things.

MR. PHILLIPS: About Aaron? There's not much about Aaron I don't know.

MAX: Is that a fact!

As MR. PHILLIPS *heads off again.*

I told you: I can't let you in there.

A beat

What kind of person won't give another person ten minutes?

There is no response from MR. PHILLIPS.

I don't like it when people won't look me in the face.

There is no response from MR. PHILLIPS. MAX *turns to the people on the line.*

Do you see this? He will not look me in the face.

Back to MR. PHILLIPS.

Are you trying to tell me I'm nothing? Is that it? Is that it, friend?

HE *walks to the wooden boxes and rights two of them.* HE *stares at* MR. PHILLIPS.

It is MR. PHILLIPS *who "blinks" first.* HE *follows* MAX *to the boxes and sits.*

MR. PHILLIPS: Who are you? What are you to Aaron?

MAX: We live in the same building. Down the hall, you know?

MR. PHILLIPS: That's all? That's it?

MAX: I look out for him.

At a quizzical look from MR. PHILLIPS.

I do. I even wash the sheets sometimes!

MR. PHILLIPS: WHAT?

MAX: Forget that. I didn't mean to say that.

MR. PHILLIPS: Aaron tells me his mother is sick. Is that true?

MAX: If that's what he said.

MR. PHILLIPS: In the hospital. Is that true?

MAX: If that's what he said.

MR. PHILLIPS: Aaron can be deceitful. He can be a liar.

MAX: True.

MR. PHILLIPS: And a thief. He has stolen money from his mother. Did you know that?

MAX: Yes, I knew that.

MR. PHILLIPS: To come here. To throw the money away on lottery tickets!

MAX: That's not so terrible, is it? It's not drugs, or guns, or–

MR. PHILLIPS: Just what he needs! A friend-in-court like Max!

MAX: Well, yes. That is what I am: a friend-in-court. He doesn't have another one that I can see.

MR. PHILLIPS: Oh, really!

MAX: Isn't that what I just said?

MR. PHILLIPS: And were you a friend-in-court at Home Depot today?

MAX: Yes. I was.

MR. PHILLIPS: Why?

MAX: He asked me to be.

MR. PHILLIPS: Why? Why did he ask you to be?

MAX: I won't tell you that.

MR. PHILLIPS: Why not?

MAX: He asked me not to.

MR. PHILLIPS: You went there to talk him out of the job, isn't that it? So you could use him here.

MAX: I never talk people out of things. I talk them into things.

MR. PHILLIPS: And to lift a few items, as well. To stuff them into those outsized pockets of yours.

MAX: *(Laughing)* There's no putting anything past you, is there, friend!

HE *reaches into his pocket and pulls out a wrench.*

It was there. I was there. Now, we're both here.

MR. PHILLIPS, *angry, starts to rise.* MAX *grabs his arm.*

You and I are going to have a coke together. That's the plan.

MR. PHILLIPS: There is no plan.

MAX: There ought to be a plan. Aaron needs us, right?

MR. PHILLIPS: Only one of us.

MAX: Okay. One of us. Which one?

MR. PHILLIPS: Not another gambler. Not a thief, who goes into a store and willy-nilly–

MAX: Watch it, okay, friend?

MONA: *(To BOBBIE)* What's willy-nilly?

BOBBIE: You got me. Did he really send you to Family Planning?

MONA: He said, "No more babies, all right?" He meant, "No more boyfriends, all right?"

BOBBIE: Oh, they hate sex! All of them.

JACK: *(Calling out* HIS *"motif")* Get this fucking show on the fucking road, all right?

BOBBIE: Jack! Only when somebody's coming. Do you see anybody coming?

MAX: (HE *puts away the wrench and watches as* MR. PHILLIPS *takes papers out of his attaché case and writes across them)* What are you writing for?

MR. PHILLIPS: Since it's fairly obvious that there is no father–

MAX: True.

MR. PHILLIPS: And since it would appear that the mother in incapable of keeping him in school or at home–

MAX: True.

MR. PHILLIPS: And since it would appear that there is only the one person down the hall, who washes the sheets–

MAX: I told you to forget that.

MR. PHILLIPS: And who encourages a 15 year-old to turn down a job, to buy lottery tickets as the one approach to his welfare–

MAX: I don't like it that you write down these things, Mr. Phillips.

MR. PHILLIPS: Is that meant to scare me? It does not scare me.

MAX: I don't like it that you raise your voice to me, Mr. Phillips.

MR. PHILLIPS: Perhaps it's time somebody did.

MAX *tries to stop him from writing.* MR. PHILLIPS *pushes* MAX'S *hand away.*

I know all I need to know.

MAX: You know nothing.

THEY *are interrupted by the arrival of* AARON *with cans/sandwich.*

Everything's all right in there? Poppy is okay?

AARON *nods.*

Good. Your job really begins now, Aaron. I want you back inside, and helping those computer experts the way we talked about it, okay?

At AARON'S *worried look.*

Everything's fine here. We are getting along very well, aren't we, Mr. Phillips?

Back to AARON.

Go to work. Go.

MR. PHILLIPS: You don't have to do anything of the kind, Aaron.

MAX: He made a promise to me.

AARON: I did, Mr. Phillips. I did.

MR. PHILLIPS: Then I'll wait for you, till you're finished.

AARON: *(Looking from face to face)* No.

MR. PHILLIPS: I will wait for you. Here. I will not leave without you. You understand?

MAX: Before you go, Aaron? See that box over there? Take it to our friend, Mona. A pregnant lady gets tired on her feet, you know?

AARON *does as he has been told.* MONA *sits on the box.* AARON, *with one last look at* MAX, *goes into the store.*

Why didn't you think of it, Mr. Phillips? Would it have killed you to consider a tired lady?

There is no response.

You don't like us, the people here at Poppy's.

Pointing to the people on the line.

You don't like them, do you?

There is no response.

Do you?

MR. PHILLIPS: You mean that pathetic little group?

MAX: No. Not pathetic.

MR. PHILLIPS: Yes. Pathetic.

MAX: They meet here, they talk, they laugh. They don't hurt anybody.

MR. PHILLIPS: *(Writing again)* Lost souls, with sweaty dollars in their hands.

MAX: "Sweaty dollars" – observant. How do you get observant like that?

HE *proceeds to eat his sandwich.*

MR. PHILLIPS: And charmed numbers they think will make them rich!

MAX: Poetic, too.

MR. PHILLIPS: The stuff dreams are made of!

MAX: "The stuff dreams are made of!" You ought to write that down.

MR. PHILLIPS *stares at him angrily.*

Well, you're probably right. I mean, 15 of the city's top 25 lottery locations are in the poorest neighborhoods. You didn't know that, right? I read it someplace.

MR. PHILLIPS: A million dollars worth of tickets sold every week, to people who ask me for money!

MAX: Actually, it's $1,600,000 a week. I read that someplace, too.

MR. PHILLIPS: *(Standing)* I won't sit on this damp box to listen to–

MAX: Oh, come on: you've tried to impress me. Let me try to impress you a little bit, why the hell not? $1,600,000 a week, can you believe it? The store owner keeps 6% of the take – I read that, too. Which comes to $96,000 a year, which sounds like a lot, but it's only the gross, you know? See? I know the word "gross." I'm not nothing, right?

MR. PHILLIPS: –with a can that's sticky and oversweet!

MAX: You know, you're right? I never noticed that about coke! You are right. Here I am trying to impress you, and you impress me instead.

MR. PHILLIPS: This is hopeless.

HE *stands again, but* MAX *gestures that* MR. PHILLIPS *must sit.*

MAX: But for somebody so observant, Mr. Phillips, don't you know the real trouble here? No? You don't understand us – Aaron, me, the people on that line. We don't live the way you do, for some time in the future, for some tomorrow. We live for now. Today. We have to.

MR. PHILLIPS: Hopeless! Hopeless!

MAX: We have to because, unless we win the lottery, how are we going to get anything?

MR. PHILLIPS: How, indeed!

MAX: No, listen. So we take a chance on a ticket with a welfare check. Sure! With a few bucks that ought to be buying food. Sure! It's important. It's necessary. On the lottery line, we get an opportunity, maybe – your kind of word. A nice car, maybe, or even a – condominium.

MR. PHILLIPS: *(Laughing)* A condominium!

MAX: Yes! A condominium! Why not? Only rich white-collars with attaché cases are supposed to get one?

MR. PHILLIPS: I have a job. That's how I got one!

MAX: No, friend, it's not a job you have. I've had jobs, and I know. It's a career you have, with benefits and pension funds and a pocket full of cash to dole out to Aaron, proving what a big man you are. It's us against them, big man, us against you, the haves versus the–

HE *laughs.*

–definitely do-not-haves. So the lottery evens it out, you know?

A beat

You're not looking at me again! You're still letting me know I'm nothing, right?

MR. PHILLIPS *slowly raises his eyes to face* MAX.

I'm more than you think, Mr. Phillips. I'm the leader type – I create opportunity. Yes, I do!

MR. PHILLIPS: We've stopped talking about Aaron, I gather.

MAX: Have we? I didn't notice.

MR. PHILLIPS: You're good at changing the subject, aren't you?

MAX: Well, well – the man thinks I'm good at something!

With a laugh.

I guess I did do that, didn't I! It's just that I want you to get this, you know? It's important. Because–

The cell phone rings, interrupting him.

Excuse me.

Into the phone.

Yes? ...Well, good...very good.

To MR. PHILLIPS.

Aaron will be finished in a few minutes.

Back to the phone.

Keep the big one in there. Send him out with the small one. Yes... the small one. Good work, guys.

HE *puts the phone away.*

Guess what?

MR. PHILLIPS: The computer experts have saved the day.

MAX: Yes: the computer experts have saved the day.

MR. PHILLIPS: They've come up with a solution, at last!

MAX: Yes: they "dug out" a solution, one might say.

MONA, BOBBIE, *and* JACK *roar with laughter at this.*

JACK: *(Calling out* HIS *"motif")* Get this fucking show on the fucking road, all right?

MAX: *(Laughing)* He understands more than you do, friend. He knows that there is money in the lottery, only you have to know how to play it right.

MAX *lowers his voice.*

See, the story around here is that our friend, Poppy, doesn't trust banks, so he keeps his take on the lottery in cash. In two carved Indian chests, what do you think of that? Somewhere in the cellar.

A beat. HE *studies* MR. PHILLIPS *rather hoping all this registers on him— a matter of pride.*

$1,000 bills in a big chest, $100 bills in a small one. Old carved Indian chests. How's that for poetic?

A beat. His pride dictates how much HE *can safely reveal.*

What I mean is: wouldn't a leader type like me, out to create opportunity, wouldn't he go down that cellar for a little while and dig for two old carved Indian chests, a big one and a little one? Well, sure he would!

A beat

You don't get it, do you? And I thought you were so observant!

A beat

I'll try again. If you found them, those two carved chests, dug them out and took them, you'd be thinking there would be consequences, right? But what if there were no consequences, what if Poppy and his whole family were here illegally: would they ever go to the police or anything? Not a chance.

A beat. HE *is becoming contemptuous of* MR. PHILLIPS' *obtuseness.*

You still don't get it. See, here's where leadership comes in. To do the digging down there in that cramped cellar, it takes someone small, you know?

A beat

And, this is where the most leadership comes in: you've got to figure out a way to keep that big family of his that lives upstairs thinking the store is open, still doing business, you see? So they won't be sticking their noses in, you see? Keep the store open but not open, you see?

A beat

You're really not getting this, are you!

A PASSERBY *comes along.*

Watch! And – listen!

MONA: *(Calling out as before)* So what's holding things up?

BOBBIE: *(Calling out as before)* Let's shake it, okay? Let's move it, okay?

To the PASSERBY.

Everything's slowed up here. The machines have broken down again.

FEMALE PASSERBY: So, when will they open again?

BOBBIE *shrugs.*

MONA: It's a computer virus.

BOBBIE: The same thing happened last week.

FEMALE PASSERBY: I always buy my tickets here.

BOBBIE: There's a place three streets down. If I could walk better, I'd go there.

JACK: *(Contributing his "motif")* Get this fucking show on the fucking road, all right?

This sends the PASSERBY *on her way, eliciting another "high five" from the "regulars."*

Now, MR. PHILLIPS *sees, at last, what* MAX'S *intriguing hints have meant all along. This "routine"* HE *has heard several times now cements it for him.*

MR. PHILLIPS: *(Quietly)* I've been had.

MAX: Well, yes. You have.

MR. PHILLIPS: I don't like being had, friend.

MAX: That's good. That's very good.

MR. PHILLIPS: *(Rising and calling out)* Aaron!

MAX: I don't think I told you to stand.

MR. PHILLIPS: Aaron!

MAX: In fact, I know I didn't tell you to stand.

MR. PHILLIPS: Come out, Aaron. You're coming with me!

MAX: *(Taking hold of* MR. PHILLIPS' *arm)* You're making me mad now, Mr. Phillips.

MR. PHILLIPS: Take that hand off me!

MAX: Real mad, friend. I'm getting real mad.

AARON *comes out of the store, a small chest hidden inside his jacket.* HE *places it near the box* MAX *has sat upon.* AARON *approaches* MAX *timidly.*

MR. PHILLIPS: Don't be frightened of him, Aaron. I–

Unseen by MR. PHILLIPS, MAX *has slipped behind him, hitting his head with the wrench.* MR. PHILLIPS, *hurt, stunned, a dazed, far-off look crossing his face, drops to his knees on the sidewalk.*

MAX: *(To* AARON*)* Put him over there.

A paralyzed AARON *doesn't move.*

I said put him over there!

AARON *props* MR. PHILLIPS *against a box. The dazed man puts his hand on the boy's arm, but can do no more.* AARON *shrinks away from him.*

Turning to the people on line.

This wasn't supposed to happen, but it did. He was getting on my nerves. Was he getting on yours?

BOBBIE: From the get-go. Right, Mona?

MONA: *(Lighting a cigarette)* From the get-go.

BOBBIE: He should know better than to be in a place like this after dark, right? If I could walk better – I mean: a person could get robbed or something!

MAX: That's just what I was thinking.

To AARON.

Bring his attaché case to me. Do what I tell you!

A frightened AARON *gets the case. There is, of course, no resistance from* MR. PHILLIPS.

Open it.

AARON *does as he has been bid.*

Is there a wallet? Bring it. Those papers, too.

AARON *does as he has been bid.* MAX *empties the wallet of its contents and throws it on the sidewalk.*

To MR. PHILLIPS.

You were in the wrong place at the wrong time, that's all, friend.

Now HE *turns to the people on line, the papers fanned out in his hand.*

You see what we are to him? Papers! That's all! Papers!

HE *slaps at* MR. PHILLIPS' *face with the papers.*

I didn't like it that you wouldn't look at me.

MR. PHILLIPS *is only able to raise his vacant eyes for a second.* MAX *throws the papers around and over him. Then,* MAX *turns to* AARON.

Bring me the chest, Aaron.

AARON *does as he has been bid.*

Good job all around, friends. We'll do another one some time soon, okay?

HE *takes a $100 bill from the chest and gives it to* MONA.

Buy something good for your boy.

MONA: A visit to a new specialist, maybe.

MAX: Then you'll need more, friend.

HE *gives her another hundred.*

MONA: *(Indicating* MR. PHILLIPS*)* He brought it on himself.

MAX: Right.

MONA: But he'll be okay, won't he?

MAX: Sure.

MONA *leaves.*

HE *takes a $100 bill from the chest and gives it to* BOBBIE.

How about you buy a cane with this.

BOBBIE: How about a pair of them?

MAX: Then you'll need this, friend.

HE *gives her another hundred.*

BOBBIE: *(Looking at* MR. PHILLIPS *as* SHE *prepares to leave)* It's only temporary amnesia, like on TV, yes?

MAX: Yes.

BOBBIE: So what the hell, then!

SHE *laughs her boisterous laugh, kisses* MAX, *and exits.*

MAX: *(Taking another $100 from the chest and giving it to* JACK*)* You're rich, Jack.

JACK: *(Calling out his "motif")* Get this fucking show on the–

MAX: *(Laughing)* You're my favorite, Jack.

HE *pats him on the back affectionately and gives him another hundred.*

It's all over for today, friend.

JACK *exits.*

To MR. PHILLIPS.

Look at what I have here, friend – lottery tickets. I thought you might want to buy them from me. No? Oh, I see: you don't have any money!

HE *laughs.*

Well, I'll give them to you. Maybe you'll get lucky.

HE *puts the tickets into* MR. PHILLIPS' *limp hand. Then* HE *turns to* AARON.

Aaron? $100 ...plus $100 more for all the digging, okay, friend? Only first–

AARON *stands looking at* MR. PHILLIPS.

Aaron? There are things to finish up inside. You have to finish them.

AARON *doesn't move.*

You get one minute, that's all.

MAX *passes by* MR. PHILLIPS' *inert figure.*

You wouldn't look at me. Why was that?

HE *heads off for the store.*

AARON *kneels before* MR. PHILLIPS *and takes his hand.* MR. PHILLIPS *stares past him, with the uncomprehending look he has worn since the beating.*

AARON: Does it hurt, Mr. Phillips?

There is no response.

I didn't know he was going to do that. Honest. He wouldn't have, only he had to.

A beat

He takes care of me. He teaches me things. He buys me shoes sometimes. I need him to take care of me, Mr. – because… because… nobody's going to give me a job, ever… because… they just aren't, that's all.

A beat

Max is good to me, with my mother being sick, and–

A beat. HE *decides to come clean.*

My mother's not in the hospital, Mr. Phillips. She has this boyfriend. He stays for a while and then he goes away and comes back again. I don't like him because… because he hits her, but she always goes with him. They always came back before. Only this time, this time, they wrote a letter to Max – he showed it to me – and they told him to take care of me because they won't be back. And Max says it will be no trouble if I do things the way he says, so it's going to be all right, you see?

HE *wipes* MR. PHILLIPS' *face with his fingers.*

Nobody else will take care of me, Mr. Phillips, because I – see – I wet the bed at night. I never told you that. I couldn't, you know? But Max says, never mind. He washes the sheets, and he never says anything, not a thing about it. You see?

A beat

Are you feeling better?

There is no response.

I asked Max to come to Home Depot, Mr. Phillips, because... because... I needed him to read the questions and fill out the papers, you know? Because I – I can't make out... some of the... I can't make out the words. I can't – I can't – I can't read!

HE *bursts into tears.*

I never told anyone. I never told you. I couldn't. You'd only say, "Everybody can read, Aaron. You're not trying." I did try, but I can't. I can't read!

A beat

I copy things sometimes, numbers, signs, things like that, even if I can't read them. When we were waiting there, at Home Depot, Max went to buy a wrench, and there was this sign. So I copied it. Here, I'll show you.

HE *takes out a crumpled piece of paper and holds it out for* MR. PHILLIPS' *inspection.*

When Max came back, he told me what the sign said: 'No Help Wanted Today.' And he said "Never mind, Aaron. I am taking care of you like I promised, and you know I have this little job for you already, and you don't have to read a thing." He is taking care of me. You see?

MR. PHILLIPS: (HE *stares at the paper* AARON *has held out to him, barely able to comprehend it. With great effort,* HE *is finally able to croak out a few words)* But this – doesn't say... Aaron, it does not say–

HE *goes quiet again.*

AARON: What, Mr. Phillips?

But there is no further sound from MR. PHILLIPS.

Will you get better, Mr. Phillips?

MR. PHILLIPS *can do nothing but look at him – no, past him – blankly.*

MAX: *(Offstage)* Aaron? I'm waiting.

AARON: (HE *pulls* MR. PHILLIPS' *coat collar around him for warmth. Then* HE *rises)* I have to go now, Mr. Phillips.

HE *begins his exit, heading slowly for the store.* HE *turns to look at* MR. PHILLIPS. *Then* HE *leaves.*

MR. PHILLIPS, *the lottery tickets still splayed in his hands, stares blankly ahead. The* YOUNG MALE PASSERBY *comes along.* HE *sees the tickets in* MR. PHILLIPS' *hand.* HE *looks to both sides, sees no one, and takes the tickets.* HE *goes off.*

THE CURTAIN FALLS
END OF PLAY

STALKING EUGENE ONEGIN

a one-act play

Stalking Eugene Onegin

setting:

The living room of an upscale apartment on Manhattan's West Side, not too many blocks from the Metropolitan Opera House.

time:

The present. A Saturday morning, just before noon, early Autumn.

characters:

GERARD PERLIS, the father, about 70.

MADDIE PERLIS, his wife, about 70.

FRANCES LAPHAM, his married daughter, about 40.

PABLO (PAUL), the assistant to the building superintendent, about 30.

AT RISE: MADDIE *sits in her wheelchair, probably under heavy sedation, "out of it."*

GERARD *kneels before her.* HE *puts fresh socks on her feet, all the while soothing her with words.* HE *would like to think she comprehends them, but the strongest certitude is that she does not.*

GERARD: Lift your feet now, my love. These will keep them dry and cool. It's such a beautiful day out there. You're going to be fine, absolutely fine. Still – in case a sudden chill should come up? We will take this blanket with us.

HE *looks at his watch.*

The taxi should be here any minute, Maddie. It's probably waiting outside for us now.

Getting her clothes ready.

And you needn't worry about the sidewalks, either. They've been putting new curb cuts on all the corners. I've seen them. You've seen them, too, sure you have! From the window. So you will have a very smooth trip out there, I promise!

Standing

There now! A blouse, a skirt and off we go! Out for the day, my lady and her hero, doing what we want to do – and we both know what that is! Nothing and nobody will stop us! What do you think of that?

There is a sudden angry knock at the door. GERARD *stops in the middle of the room.*

FRANCES: *(Offstage)* Father? Let me in.

GERARD *does not move.*

Father, don't make out you don't hear me. You do!

The doorknob is rattled several times. GERARD *remains still.*

I can let myself in, you know. I will! The super is right here with me.

PABLO: *(Offstage)* I'm not the super, Mrs. Lapham. I'm only the assistant to the super.

FRANCES: *(Offstage)* Use your key, Paul. I have this shopping bag.

The key is inserted. But the door opens only six inches.

He's got the chain on again!

Putting her mouth to the narrowly opened door.

Undo that chain, Father. I mean it – I'm not kidding. Paul is here and he's got his hacksaw.

GERARD: *(Calling out)* His name is Pablo!

FRANCES: *(Offstage)* Tell him you've got your hacksaw, Paul.

PABLO: *(Offstage)* Mr. Perlis? It's Pablo. Listen to your daughter!

In spite of doorknob rattling, there is no response from GERARD.

FRANCES: *(Offstage)* That's it! Cut the chain!

PABLO: *(Offstage)* Mr. Perlis, please? This is your third security chain. I cut this one and the board won't let you have a new one.

A beat

Mr. Perlis, please? I don't really have my hacksaw.

FRANCES: *(Offstage)* Don't tell him that! Tell him he'll get you in trouble!

PABLO: *(Offstage)* You'll get me in trouble, Mr. Perlis.

FRANCES: *(Offstage)* You will, Father, you will get him in trouble. I am going to report him to the co-op board because he has failed to remove this chain in spite of repeated requests! I swear, I will do that!

This reaches GERARD. HE *turns to* MADDIE.

GERARD: *(Whispering)* Don't worry, Maddie. We are going. You hear me? We are going!

GERARD *goes to the door and undoes the security chain.*

FRANCES *rushes in, carrying a large shopping bag.* PABLO *follows.*

PABLO: I'm sorry, Mr. Perlis. I had to.

FRANCES: That chain is to be gone today, Paul.

GERARD: His name is Pablo.

FRANCES: *(Ignoring* GERARD*)* Today! This afternoon! Do you understand?

PABLO: Yes, Mrs. Lapham.

FRANCES: How many times have I asked? Five? Fifty?

PABLO: The tenants like their chains, Mrs. Lapham. They feel safer. Ask any of them.

FRANCES: I will not ask any of them!

GERARD: We do feel safer with the chains, Frances.

FRANCES: "Safer!" How safer? There's a doorman, isn't there? There are elevator men and porters, aren't there? And that quiet one who polishes the front door all the time?

PABLO: That's Jimmy. He's a little slow, that's all.

FRANCES: Is that the point? Is that the point?

GERARD: I don't want you yelling at Pablo, Frances.

FRANCES: I will yell at him! "Safer with the chains." This is the third floor, Father, the third, not the first.

PABLO: *(Removing himself from the fray, leaning over* MADDIE *with concern)* How are you feeling today, Mrs. Perlis?

FRANCES: *(Taking plastic containers out of the shopping bag)* The apartment on the first floor would have been a whole lot cheaper for us. Did we say "Yes" to it? We said "No" to it.

GERARD: Still.

FRANCES: Never mind "still!" You think I have time for "still?" I don't have time for "still!" In exactly one hour, there will be 14 boys coming to my place. And I haven't even picked up Tommy's birthday cake!

GERARD: Don't you even want to know how your mother is feeling today?

FRANCES: Of course, I want to know how my mother is feeling today. Stop making me crazy so I can ask!

Going to MADDIE'S *side.*

How are you feeling today, Mother? You look good, very good.

PABLO *decides that this is the opportune time for him to slip out.*

(To PABLO*)* Don't even think of it!

(To MADDIE*)* You see all these containers, Mother? I've cooked some of your favorites. You know I love to cook. Remember how we used to cook together, just you and I? Of course you do.

There is no response from MADDIE, *of course.*

(To GERARD*)* Did you put the drops in her eyes?

GERARD: No.

FRANCES: And why not?

GERARD: It's not time yet, that's why not.

PABLO *tries to slip out again. This time,* FRANCES *stops him with a mere look.*

PABLO: *(Hurriedly turning his attention to* MADDIE*)* You see what a beautiful day it is, Mrs. Perlis? Would you like me to open the windows for you?

FRANCES: *(To* PABLO*)* The windows stay closed. There's a wind.

(To GERARD*)* What do you mean, "It's not time yet?" "Mid-afternoon, even-numbered days."

GERARD: I know "mid-afternoon." This is not mid-afternoon. This is early afternoon.

FRANCES: Which means you forgot. It wouldn't surprise me if you've forgotten where her eye drops are.

GERARD: I do not forget important things, Frances.

PABLO: *(Meekly)* I really have to go.

FRANCES *merely holds up her hand to indicate* PABLO *is not to go.*

FRANCES: *(To* GERARD*)* You don't forget important things! I suppose the phone was not off the hook all day yesterday? I suppose someone – guess who? – did not forget to hang it up? I suppose someone else – guess who? – did not have to ring Paul and ask him to hang it up?

GERARD: His name is Pablo.

PABLO: I didn't mind, Mrs. Lapham.

As his cell phone rings.

Ah! The inspector is here for the boiler.

FRANCES: Turn that off.

PABLO: But–

FRANCES: Turn it off!

PABLO *turns it off.*

You are to get your hacksaw, Paul, and be back here in fifteen minutes. Not twenty minutes, fifteen! And no getting involved with other jobs.

PABLO: I won't need a hacksaw, Mrs. Lapham. Only a–

FRANCES: Whatever! The chain will be off before I leave, or I will report you to the co-op board again.

PABLO: *(About to exit)* Yes, Mrs. Lapham.

FRANCES: Did I say I was finished? I did not! Let us discuss the rule that I am to be called the second, the very second, my father asks someone to get a taxi for him. You've been told, Paul, don't say you haven't because I've told you.

PABLO: But we do that, Mrs. Lapham.

GERARD: Why would I ask for a taxi, Frances?

FRANCES: Why? Why? You think I don't know?

(To PABLO*)* "We do that, Mrs. Lapham, we do that, Mrs. Lapham." I suppose that was not a taxi in front of the building when I got here?

PABLO: I don't call for the taxis. It's the doorman's job.

GERARD: What makes you think it was for me?

FRANCES: Because I asked! Nobody in this building listens, nobody! It's lucky I got here when I did, or God knows where they'd be now.

GERARD: Right here is where we'd be.

FRANCES: *(Firmly and flatly to* GERARD*)* You were planning to take her out. I need not ask where!

GERARD: I was not planning to–

FRANCES: What's the opera today?

PABLO: *(Uneasily)* May I be excused, please?

FRANCES: *(To* PABLO*)* What's the opera today?

PABLO: The opera? You're asking me?

FRANCES: Yes, I'm asking you.

PABLO: The opera! How would I know?

FRANCES: Oh, who can believe any of you! You will be up here in ten minutes to remove the chain. You will.

PABLO: Yes, Mrs. Lapham.

FRANCES: And to hear some new rules.

GERARD: What new rules?

FRANCES: New rules I should have made a long time ago.

PABLO: *(Going to* MADDIE*)* Have a good day, Mrs. Perlis.

Whispering to GERARD.

They're in there.

GERARD: *(Whispering)* What?

PABLO: *(Indicating a drawer and whispering)* The eye drops. In there.

FRANCES: *(Working at the containers again)* What's that whispering?

PABLO: Nothing.

FRANCES: You think I'm some sort of monster, Paul.

PABLO: No, Mrs. Lapham.

FRANCES: I am not a monster.

PABLO: Yes, Mrs. Lapham. I mean, no, Mrs. Lapham.

FRANCES: All right, then.

PABLO, *happy to get out of there, exits quickly.*

Now FRANCES *stares at* GERARD *rather sadly.*

More softly

What about you? Do you think I'm some sort of monster?

GERARD: I don't think that at all, Frances.

Now FRANCES *and* GERARD *look at each other a long time.*

FRANCES: *(Genuinely)* Thank you for the birthday card for Tommy. And for the check. It was nice of you.

GERARD: Would I forget such an important thing?

FRANCES: *(Not unkindly)* You were getting ready to go to the opera this afternoon. Admit it.

GERARD: I–

Quietly

Yes.

FRANCES: What is the opera today?

GERARD: *Eugene Onegin.*

FRANCES: *Eugene Onegin.*

A soft sardonic laugh.

She can barely see. She doesn't hear at all that I can make out. Her mind is God knows where. But you'll stalk *Eugene Onegin*!

GERARD: It is her all-time favorite.

FRANCES: You mean it was her all-time favorite.

GERARD: I mean it is her all-time favorite. Afterwards–

FRANCES: Don't tell me "afterwards." There is no "afterwards."

GERARD: *(Firmly)* Afterwards I was going to take her to dinner at–

FRANCES: Opera! Dinner! I don't believe this! Assuming you could get her dressed, assuming you could get that wheelchair into the elevator, what about the front steps? Did you even think about that?

GERARD: The staff is nice. They would help.

FRANCES: Of course, they're nice. Of course, they would help. George showers them with cash every holiday season, doesn't he?

GERARD: The cabbies would help, too. All you have to do is ask.

FRANCES: The cabbies! So the cabbies suddenly know what they're doing! She bled for two hours after the last one helped! Forget it – there will be no more cabbies!

There is no response from an increasingly sad GERARD.

Softer now.

Father, I'm not trying to be mean. I'm not.

GERARD: I know you're not.

FRANCES: Then co-operate with me.

GERARD: I do co-operate with you.

FRANCES: Think how willingly George pays half the maintenance here. That is not a small thing.

GERARD: Who said it was a small thing?

FRANCES: The visiting nurse, too, don't forget that. Five days a week.

GERARD: Four days a week.

FRANCES: Four days a week. That's remarkable generosity, remarkable.

GERARD: It is, Frances. It is remarkable.

FRANCES: Do you hear a word from him?

GERARD: Never. Not a word.

FRANCES: Maybe you think you and Mother are my only worry these days? You should see how George looks lately when he comes home from work.

GERARD: He shouldn't put in such hours.

FRANCES: Tell him that! What does he ask for in return?

GERARD: Nothing. Nothing at all.

FRANCES: You're being sarcastic.

GERARD: Why would I be sarcastic? He is a generous man, too generous.

FRANCES: What do I ask for in return?

There is no response from GERARD.

What I ask for in return is that my mother and father should live, should continue to live, in ease here, in this beautiful apartment. What I ask for in return is that they show some sense about what they can and can no longer do. What I ask for in return is that they not plan crazy things behind my back.

GERARD: *(Sadly)* We saw *Eugene Onegin* on our honeymoon, Frances.

FRANCES: That was 100 years ago! You can't have that back, not that, not "afterwards," not any of it! You'll stay here this afternoon. You'll sit by the windows and look at that gorgeous sky.

GERARD: *(Calmly)* We're prisoners, then.

FRANCES: *(Really hurt by this)* Is that what you think?

GERARD: Yes! I do!

FRANCES: *(Bursting into tears)* Don't say that, Father! It isn't fair!

SHE *looks at her watch.*

Where is that Paul?

A beat. SHE *looks at the containers she has brought.* SHE *rises and goes to them.*

Look at this! You get me so distracted, I forget why I'm here.

SHE *picks up containers and refers to the labels on them.*

These are your meals for the week. This one goes into the refrigerator now – it's tonight's dinner. Meat loaf. The rest will be in the freezer.

Realizing GERARD *is not paying attention.*

Look at me! This is important! I've marked each of the containers: Sunday, Monday. Are you paying attention?

GERARD: I know the days of the week, Frances.

FRANCES: Is that the point? Is that the point? No! The point is that these meals are in special order. There's a day between meat and poultry – a vegetarian dish, delicious but low-calorie. It's better for you both.

GERARD: And if I happen accidentally not to skip a day between meat and poultry, the sky falls?

FRANCES: See what you're like? Do you see what you're like? Because you're disappointed about today, you take that disappointment out on–

GERARD: Frances! I am not going to read labels when I sit down to eat. I am not going to skip days when I sit down to eat. I am going to chew. I am going to enjoy. What do you think about that?

FRANCES: *(Looking squarely at him and then suddenly bursting into laughter)* Do you hear yourself? Do you?

GERARD: *(Smiling)* Yes. I do. Am I impossible?

FRANCES: That's just what you are! Impossible!

GERARD *and* FRANCES *join in laughter which eventually subsides; then,* THEY *share a moment of quiet affection.*

GERARD *notices* FRANCES *looking at her watch.*

GERARD: Pablo gets busy. Everybody has a job for him.

FRANCES: *(Tenderly)* You cut yourself shaving, you know.

GERARD: I know.

FRANCES: *(Pointing to his chin)* There. And there. And there. Doesn't it hurt?

GERARD: No.

FRANCES: The visiting nurse would shave you.

GERARD: The visiting nurse comes for your mother, not for me.

FRANCES: Nevertheless, she would shave you. All you'd have to do is ask.

GERARD: No one is going to shave me but me, Frances.

FRANCES: *(Tenderly)* All right, Father.

A long beat.

Do you remember when you took me to my first opera?

GERARD: Of course, I do.

FRANCES: Do you remember what the opera was?

GERARD: Of course, I do.

FRANCES: What was it?

GERARD: *Der Rosenkavalier.*

FRANCES: Right! I remember everything about that day, everything! The date, the weather, what I had on, what Mother had on. I wore my wine velvet dress and Mother wore that blue dress with the beads on the jacket. Do you remember that dress?

GERARD: Of course, I remember that dress.

FRANCES: I remember the taxi ride. You wouldn't let me sit between you. I had to sit on Mother's side.

GERARD *nods, affecting a cough, the reason for the seating arrangement.*

You remember, too! You had a cold. You held your hand up to your mouth the whole time so I wouldn't catch it. Oh, yes, I do remember everything. When the curtain went up, there was this countess–

GERARD: The Marschallin.

FRANCES: The Marschallin! She was the loveliest lady I had ever seen. She had a young servant. What was his name?

GERARD: Octavian.

FRANCES: Octavian! And there was a rose, a silver rose! It was so beautiful, it made me cry! Oh, how I wanted to see that silver rose again! How I begged you to take me again!

GERARD: Which I did.

FRANCES: Yes, you did, you and Mother and I, again, off to see *Der Rosenkavalier* a second time. Afterwards–

GERARD: *(Sadly)* Afterwards. That wonderful restaurant your mother loved so much is gone now.

Looking straight at FRANCES, *pleadingly.*

But there are new restaurants, Frances. It's only six blocks to the Opera House, Frances.

FRANCES: *(Not unkindly)* It might as well be six hundred blocks. You know I'm right. Admit I'm right.

GERARD *goes silent.* THEY *look away from each other. The doorbell rings.*

Finally!

Calling out.

Come in, Paul.

PABLO *enters with his own key, carrying his tools.*

I don't see a hacksaw, Paul.

PABLO: I don't need one.

HE *holds up some tools.*

Only these, honest.

FRANCES: Hurry, then. I've really got to go.

PABLO: Yes, Mrs. Lapham.

HE *sets to work quietly on the security chain.*

FRANCES: *(To* GERARD*)* So, Father, since you know the opera is out, you won't mind giving me the tickets. We won't fight about it, will we?

GERARD: *(Defeated)* On the desk.

FRANCES *picks up an envelope from the desk.*

FRANCES: When did you send for them?

GERARD: Two months ago.

FRANCES: She was back in the hospital two months ago.

GERARD: I gave her something to look forward to.

FRANCES: I very much doubt that, since she knew nothing and heard nothing and saw nothing. Not that it is so much different today.

Returning to her seat, SHE *feels the envelope.*

If you were any other father in the world, I wouldn't have to do this, would I! But these could be cut-up newspapers like last time. Or cardboard, like the time before that.

Finding the tickets.

Well! A little honesty, at last!

Examining the tickets.

Way up there?

GERARD: They were the only tickets left.

FRANCES: And now you're going to tell me that people would have helped you to get to these seats?

GERARD: Yes, they would have.

FRANCES: I don't believe that for a second.

GERARD: What does it matter?

FRANCES: Correct. What does it matter?

Removing the tickets from the envelope.

If you were any other father in the world, I wouldn't have to do this, either!

SHE *puts the tickets into her pocket.*

Don't think for one minute I like doing this. I don't like it! Maybe it will convince you to stop ordering tickets you can't use.

Looking at her watch.

Before I go, I want to make sure Mother gets her drops. Get them for me, please.

GERARD: What?

FRANCES: You do know where they are? You do remember where you've put them?

GERARD: Yes, I remember where I've put them.

FRANCES: Then get them, please.

Kneeling before MADDIE.

Mother? This is Frances, your daughter, Frances. I can't stay long and I'll tell you why.

Unseen by FRANCES, PABLO *has stopped his work to signal again where the drops are.* GERARD *gets them from a drawer and gives them to* FRANCES.

Tenderly to MADDIE.

Today is Tommy's birthday. He is 14 years old; can you believe it? 14 years old, and 14 boys coming to a party. So, you see, I can't stay. Now I'm going to put these drops into your eyes. Two drops, then we wait, then two more drops. You'll feel cool and refreshed.

SHE *puts the drops into* MADDIE'S *eyes.*

There we are. There we are!

With a tissue, SHE *wipes* MADDIE'S *cheeks. Then* SHE *turns to* GERARD.

Remember, Father: you have to do this again at–

GERARD: 9 PM.

FRANCES: And you won't forget? I know: you won't forget the important things! See? I listen to you. Why won't you listen to me? Promise me, promise me, that you'll keep her quiet this afternoon. She looks so tired. Make her take a nap.

GERARD: I always do, don't I?

FRANCES: No. You don't always. It wouldn't be a bad idea for you to nap, too. You're exhausted.

GERARD: I'm not exhausted.

FRANCES: I see it in your face.

GERARD: *(Angrily)* You do not see it in my face!

FRANCES: All right!

More quietly.

All right, then.

Turning to MADDIE, SHE *takes* MADDIE'S *hand and strokes her own cheek with it tenderly.*

Remember when you used to do this, Mother? You said your hand was magic and could wipe away any little tear I had? And it was magic, and it did wipe my tears away. Now I'll stroke your cheek with my hand.

SHE *strokes* MADDIE'S *cheek.*

Because you can use a magic hand today, right? Sure you can!

GERARD *and* PABLO *watch this tender moment intensely. Finally,* FRANCES *rises.*

PABLO: All done, Mrs. Lapham.

FRANCES: Let me have the chain, please, Paul.

PABLO *brings the chain to* FRANCES.

Do you know why I have to be so cautious? Because I'm not sure I can trust anyone in this building, even you. Sometimes I think you are too much on my father's side, too ready to–

PABLO: Me, Mrs. Lapham?

FRANCES: Yes, you!

PABLO: Not me, Mrs. Lapham.

FRANCES: "Not me, Mrs. Lapham, not me, Mrs. Lapham." Do I have your promise, then, your absolute promise, that you will not put back a chain, no matter what he says?

PABLO: Yes, Mrs. Lapham.

FRANCES: I am going to hold you to that, Paul.

PABLO: *(Preparing to exit)* Yes, Mrs. Lapham.

FRANCES: I'm not finished. I mentioned some new rules. Look at me please, Paul. My father and mother are not to get into the passenger elevators this afternoon without you calling me immediately.

GERARD: You don't have to do this, Frances.

FRANCES: *(Ignoring* GERARD*)* If they try, you, you personally, are to call me. You know how quickly I can be here.

GERARD: Why would we get into elevators? We don't have a place to go any more!

FRANCES: *(Ignoring* GERARD*)* Repeat after me, Paul: "Mr. and Mrs. Perlis are not to enter the passenger elevators this afternoon."

GERARD: So what are we? Under house arrest?

FRANCES: *(Ignoring* GERARD*)* Say it!

PABLO: "Mr. and Mrs. Perlis are not to enter the passenger elevators"–

FRANCES: "–either of the passenger elevators this afternoon."

PABLO: "either of the passenger elevators this afternoon."

FRANCES: "Or any afternoon."

GERARD: Any afternoon?

PABLO: Any afternoon?

FRANCES: "Unless Mrs. Lapham is called immediately and can go downstairs with them." Do you understand?

GERARD: We are under house arrest, then.

FRANCES: *(Ignoring* GERARD*)* Which doesn't mean the old rule about the taxi doesn't apply, Paul. It also applies.

PABLO: I don't call for taxis, Mrs. Lapham. The doorman calls for–

FRANCES *withers him with an impatient look.*

"No taxis, either."

FRANCES: If any of the staff, the doorman, anyone, including the one who does nothing at all but polish the front door–

PABLO: That's Jimmy–

FRANCES: *(Holding her hand up to stop him)* Whatever his name is, if any of them calls a taxi for my father, I am to be notified.

PABLO: Yes, Mrs. Lapham.

FRANCES: Immediately! Two more minutes today and they'd have been gone!

PABLO: Yes, Mrs. Lapham.

FRANCES: Okay, then. Okay.

PABLO: *(Happy to exit)* I'm leaving now, Mr. Perlis.

Going to MADDIE.

Goodbye, Mrs. Perlis.

In his zeal to leave, HE *nearly forgets the toolbox.* HE *comes back, retrieves it, and scoots out as fast as he can.*

FRANCES: *(A beat)* Tell me I have put my trust in the right person, Father.

There is no response from GERARD.

Tell me I have–

GERARD *turns from her.*

I know this is not the afternoon you might want, Father, but–

GERARD: Just go, okay?

FRANCES: *(Hurt,* SHE *goes to* MADDIE *and kneels before her)* I know this is not the afternoon you might want either, Mother. But it is the afternoon you have to have. It's nobody's fault. It's the way things are. You see?

SHE *studies* MADDIE'S *face, then with quiet pain turns to* GERARD.

She belongs in a nursing home.

GERARD: No. She doesn't.

FRANCES: Everybody knows it. You know it.

GERARD: There will be no nursing home, Frances.

FRANCES: Assisted living. Something!

GERARD: They're all nursing homes, whatever you call them. We don't want them and we don't need them. As long as I've got my arms and legs, I can do for her the way I've been doing for her.

FRANCES: *(Calmly)* All right, Father, all right.

Taking the tickets from her pocket and going to MADDIE.

Mother? I know how much you loved the opera. Especially *Eugene Onegin.* I do remember that. And if I thought you could hear it, or understand one word of it–

GERARD: She can understand it.

FRANCES: *(Ignoring* GERARD*)* –or would even know where you were, or what you were there for, I'd take you myself, I would!

GERARD: *(Coming to* MADDIE *and kneeling before her)* Frances, look into her eyes! If I tell her she's going to the Opera, a light comes into her eyes. I see it!

FRANCES: *(Holding* MADDIE'S *face in her hands)* Opera, Mother? *Eugene Onegin,* Mother? The ball? The mazurka? Tatiana writing her letter?

(To GERARD*)* There's no light in her eyes, Father. It's something you've made up.

GERARD: There is, Frances, there is! A spark, a glow, a–

FRANCES: *(Calmly)* There is no spark, Father. There is no glow. She doesn't know who she is. She doesn't know who you are or who I am.

(To MADDIE*)* Do you know me, Mother? Do you?

(To GERARD*)* There is nothing in her eyes, Father. There is nothing.

GERARD *stands mute. There is no sign of any kind from* MADDIE. FRANCES *rises slowly, in deep pain.* SHE *tears up the tickets into little pieces and throws them to the floor.*

I'll be home in 10 minutes. And the second I'm there, I am going to call. You'll be here. You'd better be here. Do you hear me?

GERARD: I hear you.

FRANCES: If you were any other father in the world, I wouldn't have to do this, either.

SHE *picks up the pieces from the floor and puts them in a wastebasket.* SHE *smiles.*

I wouldn't put it past you to try taping all the pieces together. I do have to go now. There are 14 boys coming to the apartment in exactly–

GERARD: You've already told me that, Frances. You have trouble remembering things these days.

FRANCES: *(Laughing in spite of herself)* What am I going to do with you? You are impossible! You are!

Kissing him affectionately, SHE *leaves.*

GERARD *stands quietly for a moment, until he is sure she is gone.* HE *locks the door and returns to* MADDIE.

GERARD: *(Jubilantly)* Hah! You didn't think she was going to keep us from the opera today, did you, Maddie? She is not! We will outwit her. We have outwitted her! You saw her rip up those tickets? We've got two more, haven't we! We sent for four tickets, Maddie, four, remember? Sure, you do! You sat right at my side when I wrote the check! And you were here when I got the tickets and when I put two of them in a place where she'd never look, where I'd be sure to find them the moment I wanted them! Now – where are they?

As HE *talks to* MADDIE, *he looks from drawer to drawer.*

In this drawer, I think, Maddie. No? This one? No? Just give me a minute and I'll remember. I do not forget the important things, isn't that so, my love? And this is important!

A courageous laugh, to mask increasing anxiety.

Everything about *Eugene Onegin* is important, isn't it? It is. It is!

Searching with increasing desperation.

Here? No. Well, then, here.

But opening drawer after drawer, HE *finds no tickets.*

You may have to help me on this, Maddie. I may not be able to do this alone. I can't do everything by myself, you know.

A bit of anger.

It isn't fair to ask me to do everything by myself. Nobody can do everything!

The anger dissolves into fear as HE *continues the search.*

Help me, Maddie! You have to help me!

There are no more places for him to search. HE *bursts into tears.* HE *sits.*

I tried, Maddie. You saw. I did try. I can't always find ways to fight for us.

HE *lets his age overcome him.*

You don't suppose Frances is right, Maddie? You don't suppose we can't have afternoons at the opera the way we used to? Am I getting too old, Maddie? Do you forgive me for getting too old?

A long beat. HE *takes* MADDIE'S *hand.*

I'm a little tired, my lady, just a little. I'll rest now, is that okay? A quick rest and I'll be as good as new.

Still holding MADDIE'S *hand,* HE *lies down on the couch.*

A long beat; then the doorbell rings. GERARD *doesn't answer it. The doorbell rings again. Finally,* PABLO *lets himself in.*

PABLO: *(Going to* GERARD *and whispering)* Mr. Perlis? Mr. Perlis? It's late. You should be getting ready.

GERARD: *(Eyes still closed)* What, Pablo?

PABLO: Come on, get up. There isn't much time. You have to get Mrs. Perlis dressed.

GERARD: What for?

PABLO: What for? You know what for!

GERARD: We're not going, Pablo. We can't.

PABLO: Of course you can! Why can't you?

GERARD: Too old, Pablo. We're both too old for afternoons like we used to have.

PABLO: You have that wrong, Mr. Perlis. It's going to the opera that will keep you young! I can't see opera for beans myself – I'd fall asleep in two minutes. But if opera is what you like, opera is what you do! You have to go!

There is no response from GERARD. PABLO *picks up a piece of ticket from the floor.*

She ripped up the tickets like you said she would! Hah!

Beginning to laugh, then catching himself mid-laugh.

I mean no disrespect.

A beat

That was some idea, some great idea, to order four tickets!

GERARD: *(Eyes still closed)* Did I do that, Pablo?

PABLO: Of course, you did that! How can she stop you when you get a great idea like that?

GERARD: Then I didn't imagine it?

PABLO: No, you didn't imagine it!

Laughing

Four tickets, in case she rips up two of them!

GERARD: You're sure, Pablo?

PABLO: Didn't I mail the order for you myself?

GERARD: *(Opening his eyes and sitting up)* But, Pablo, if I did ... if I – no, it's no good. See – I'm too old.

PABLO: Why?

GERARD: Because I did something dumb with the other two. I've lost them, Pablo.

PABLO: Mr. Perlis! Mr. Perlis, you gave me the two extra tickets. For safekeeping.

HE *produces two tickets.*

See?

GERARD: Did I do that?

PABLO: Yes!

GERARD: *(With renewed hope)* Yes! Yes, I did!

PABLO: And you'd have remembered it, too, except it was such a morning with the security chain and your daughter yelling – I mean no disrespect – and all.

GERARD: *(To* MADDIE*)* Did you hear, Maddie? I did order four tickets! I–

Sitting again.

No, Pablo. I can't do it. I can't let it happen to you.

PABLO: Let what happen to me?

GERARD: We can't go down the elevator. She'll report you, you know she will.

PABLO: Mr. Perlis, she can't report me. Don't you remember the words?

GERARD: The words?

PABLO: She said: "They are not to enter the passenger elevators." She said, "Either of the passenger elevators." She pointed right at the elevator banks.

GERARD: You see? You'll be in trouble with–

PABLO: She did not say: "They are not to enter the service elevator," did she? She did not say, "Don't take them to the basement and walk them out the service entrance," did she?

GERARD: *(Laughing)* No, she did not say–

The laughter stops abruptly.

She'll know. She'll know.

PABLO: How will she know? I'll put Jimmy on the service elevator.

HE *indicates with a finger to his head that Jimmy sometimes has confused brain waves.*

He won't figure out what we've done for a week, poor guy.

GERARD: *(A beat as he grasps the possibility)* What about the taxi? If I try to get another taxi, the doorman will call her.

PABLO: It's a beautiful day, Mr. Perlis. Look.

HE *opens a window.*

You'll walk Mrs. Perlis in her wheelchair. A few blocks to the opera in wonderful sunshine! And a good head start, too!

GERARD: Head start?

PABLO: The service entrance is one block closer to the Opera House, right?

GERARD: Right!

Stopping in his tracks.

Frances is going to phone here in 5 minutes.

PABLO: So it's off the hook again.

GERARD: She'll come.

PABLO: Is it four boys or fourteen boys coming to her apartment this afternoon?

GERARD: *(Jubilantly)* Fourteen!

PABLO: So there! I'll set it up – leave it to me.

GERARD: You'd do all this, Pablo?

PABLO: My dad was a nut about fishing. Would I have wanted him to give it up while he lived?

GERARD: *(To* MADDIE*)* We will go! We will go, Maddie!

To PABLO *as* HE *gathers* MADDIE'S *clothes.*

There's food in the refrigerator, Pablo. I want you to take it.

PABLO: Oh, I couldn't do that, Mr. Perlis.

GERARD: I want you to, Pablo, and I'll tell you why: Mrs. Perlis and I are going to have an afternoon exactly like the ones we used to have, aren't we, Maddie? We're going to go out to dinner afterwards!

PABLO: Hey – great! Promise me you'll do that and I'll take the food.

HE *opens the refrigerator.*

"Saturday: meat loaf." I like meat loaf.

GERARD: Take "Sunday" from the freezer. Sunday is a vegetable dish. I hate it.

PABLO: *(Getting the container from the freezer)* I'll give "Sunday" to Jimmy. He likes everything. Get Mrs. Perlis ready now, okay?

About to leave.

Oh – you want me to take the phone off the hook?

GERARD: I'll remember.

PABLO *starts to exit.*

Hey, Pablo!

PABLO: Yes?

GERARD: You've forgotten something!

PABLO: *(Thinking, realizing he has the tickets, then laughing,* HE *puts the tickets down near the phone)* Good for you!

(To MADDIE*)* You have a wonderful time, Mrs. Perlis. Both of you have a wonderful time.

PABLO *exits.* GERARD *kneels before the wheelchair.* HE *proceeds to dress her – shoes, blouse, wraparound skirt.*

When he must, HE *makes her stand. At such times,* SHE *is entirely dependent on him, trusting and loving: perhaps a bit – only a bit – of that "light" shines out of her eyes as* SHE *hears or does not hear his soothing words.*

GERARD: On our way, my lady. We are on our way! It's going to be wonderful. You remember what the Opera House looks like? Sure you do: all that red carpeting and that grand staircase and the gold trim? And the chandeliers, you remember them! You said they looked like clusters of stars, and, of course, that's what they are meant to look like! Do you remember how they climb slowly up to the ceiling? You love that! Oh, Maddie! I see something in your eyes! I do! You are so happy to be going out with me this afternoon. You are!

Laughing

You see? As long as I remember the important things like the chandeliers that climb to the ceiling, you and I have absolutely nothing to worry about, ever.

HE *looks around.* HE *is supposed to do something.*

There's something I'm supposed to do? What is it? Oh, I know!

HE *picks up the tickets from the table.*

They won't let us into the Opera House without these, will they?

HE *pockets the tickets.*

Our forgetful friend, Pablo, nearly went off with them, what do you think of that?

HE *gets a light blanket and adjusts it over her.*

Just in case a sudden chill comes up, Maddie. There. You remember how *Eugene Onegin* goes, don't you, my love? They're making jam in the kitchen when the curtain goes up, the young girls, Tatiana and – I forget the other one's name.

And then Tatiana sees Eugene and she falls in love with him and writes a letter, a beautiful letter. Oh, you love that letter, I know! And then… and then… what happens, Maddie? Yes, I know! She gives the letter to the Marschallin's servant, Octavian, and–

HE *adjusts a light sweater on her arms.*

–that's it, the sleeve goes over your arm this way – and Octavian brings Tatiana a silver rose. A silver rose, Maddie – isn't that a beautiful thing to think about?

HE *looks around the room. Then* HE *remembers the phone.*

Ahh! Phone off the hook! Done! Yes, I see in your eyes, Maddie, that you think a silver rose is a very beautiful thing! The rose is for Eugene, you know, for Eugene Onegin. Tatiana gives him the silver rose because she loves him so! As long as I remember important things like that, nothing can stop us, ever!

GERARD *and* MADDIE *start out,* GERARD *gently pushing the wheelchair.*

We are going to have a lovely walk, Maddie, you and I, just you and I, right to the beautiful Opera House, and to your favorite opera. Oh, Maddie, you do hear, you do understand. I know you do, my love. I know you do!

HE *pushes* MADDIE *towards the door as the lights go down.*

THE CURTAIN FALLS
END OF PLAY

TRAILER TRASH

a dramatic monologue

Trailer Trash

setting:
A cramped trailer, sparsely furnished.
A telephone and a chair are the only props required.

time:
The present, late at night.

character:
LOU-ANNE, mid-thirties, poor, one of life's castoffs.

AT RISE: The lights come up on a woman, with a bandaged right eye, holding on to a telephone. SHE *waits; then, after a beat.*

LOU-ANNE

Hello, Suzanne?... Is this Suzanne?... I can't believe I'm actually talking to Suzanne! I just love you, Suzanne, and I just love your home shopping show! Well, thank you, but, you see, if you wave, I won't be able to see it, anyway. Wouldn't you just know it, though! My TV set is on the blink tonight, this very night when I finally got through to you?... On top of which, this eye infection! ...Yes, fate's naughty tricks, you're right!... Well, I just wanted you to know I got my kanchanarabi – is that the right way to pronounce it? ...It is? ...My kanchanarabi ruby ring from Siam, and I love it! I'm wearing it now...It's 3 AM where I am, but I'm wearing my ring, and I will never take it off!

SHE *holds out her hand to examine the ring.*

It's so big, and so – pure-looking. It's just like a piece of glass!... Oh, no! I didn't mean it that way, no... It is, oh, yes, the buy of a lifetime. I have a few of your rings, a lot of them actually, Suzanne. You should see my credit card. It looks like the national debt, ha, ha!... What? Well, no, I buy them myself because my husband sort of doesn't approve of me having all this stuff, you know?... What?... He's asleep. Well, after all, it is 3 AM, some people do sleep, ha, ha!... No, it's not a house. It's a trailer. We live in this trailer park, the Checkerberry Trailer Park... Yes, it is nice...

A bit frantically.

Oh, no, Suzanne, don't go, don't hang up. You can't hang up. I want to talk to you just a little bit more. I need to talk to you... I shouldn't buy another thing, Suzanne, but I will because, as you always say, you're only around once, just once, and – wait. Wait! Don't go, Suzanne. I haven't told you how happy I am with your products. Yes, I am. I get teased, actually, because I buy so many of them. More than teased, Suzanne.

Starting to break down.

We had a fight, actually, my husband and I, just before I called you. He broke the TV, actually, and then he – he left because I... well, he called me a spendthrift, ha, ha, a cheap floozy and a spendthrift, which is so dumb, because how can you be cheap and a spendthrift, right, ha, ha? And, besides, like you always say, Suzanne – it's not a question, right, not a question of how much you spend, but how much you save, right?... He's left me, Suzanne. He hit me, and then he.... No, don't go, please, don't hang up. I'm your A#1 customer, why would you hang up on me when – Suzanne? Suzanne?

A long beat.

Who are you?... I don't want to talk to no assistant, I want Suzanne... Why can't I? Why? I buy all her crap, don't I?

Now getting very desperate.

No. Don't hang up. What's your name? ...Marjorie? That's a nice name. I want to take back what I just said. It isn't crap, it isn't. It does make me happy. It keeps me happy to buy from Suzanne... Listen, Marjorie – I know you're all very busy there. I mean, you have a lot to do and everything, but Marjorie? Would you at least tell Suzanne I said goodbye? Tell her I love her and I love her rings and I love her program. And, Marjorie–

Another beat. More quietly now.

Can I call you again? Because, you see, Marjorie, I don't sleep well, and sometimes I get frightened late at night... I don't know why.... I can? Oh, Marjorie, thanks so much, that's so good of you because I need someone to talk to sometimes, okay?... Oh, thanks, Marjorie, thanks. I love you, too. Oh, by the way: my name is – hello? Are you there? Hello?

SHE *hangs up the phone and looks at the ring on her finger.* SHE *takes the bandage away from her face, revealing a big blue bruise.* SHE *stares blankly into space as the lights come down.*

THE CURTAIN FALLS
END OF PLAY

www.ingramcontent.com/pod-product-compliance
Lightning Source LLC
Chambersburg PA
CBHW070808100426
42742CB00012B/2290